LiTTLE GUiDES

Bugs

Bugs

Consultant Editor
Dr Noel Tait

FOG CITY PRESS

Published by Fog City Press
814 Montgomery Street
San Francisco, CA 94133 USA

ISBN 1 740893 46 8

Color reproduction by SC (Sang Choy) International Pte Ltd
Printed by SNP Leefung Printers Ltd
Printed in China

A Weldon Owen Production
Produced using arkiva retrieval technology
For further information, contact arkiva@weldonowen.com.au

FOG CITY PRESS
Chief Executive Officer: John Owen
President: Terry Newell
Publisher: Sheena Coupe
Creative Director: Sue Burk
Project Editor: Jessica Cox
Series Design: Nika Markovtzev
Project Designers: Hilda Mendham, Heather Menzies
Editorial Coordinator: Irene Mickaiel
Production Managers: Louise Mitchell, Caroline Webber
Production Coordinator: Monique Layt
Sales Manager: Emily Jahn
Vice President International Sales: Stuart Laurence

Contents

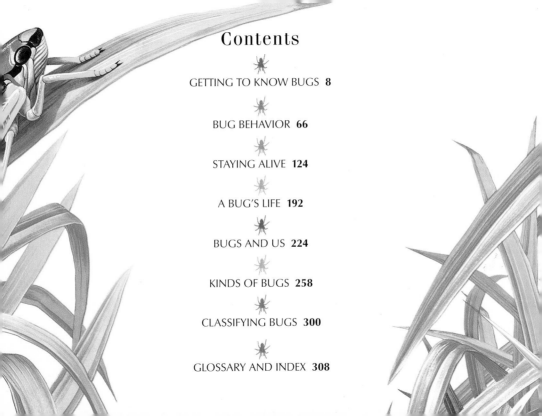

GETTING TO KNOW BUGS

Insects

Insects belong to a group of animals called arthropods, which also includes spiders, scorpions, crabs, and millipedes. All of these creatures have a tough outer shell, called an exoskeleton, instead of an internal skeleton. Insects as a group have their own unique characteristics—these are labeled on the bee.

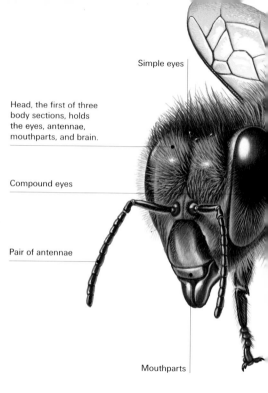

Simple eyes

Head, the first of three body sections, holds the eyes, antennae, mouthparts, and brain.

Compound eyes

Pair of antennae

Mouthparts

TRUE BUGS
Even though we call many arthropods "bugs," true bugs are a group of insects that have a piercing beak instead of jaws.

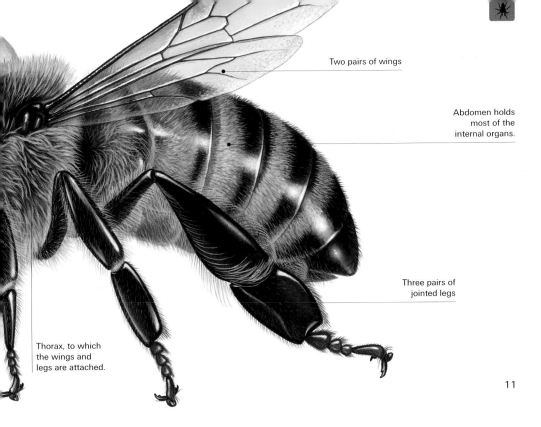

Two pairs of wings

Abdomen holds
most of the
internal organs.

Three pairs of
jointed legs

Thorax, to which
the wings and
legs are attached.

11

Spiders

At first glance, it is easy to confuse insects and spiders, because they both have exoskeletons and jointed limbs. But there the resemblance ends. Spiders are part of a group of arthropods called arachnids, which includes scorpions, harvestmen, mites, and ticks. Spiders are all predators.

SPIDER LOOK-ALIKE

Although this harvestman looks a lot like a spider, it is another type of arachnid.

Four pairs of jointed legs

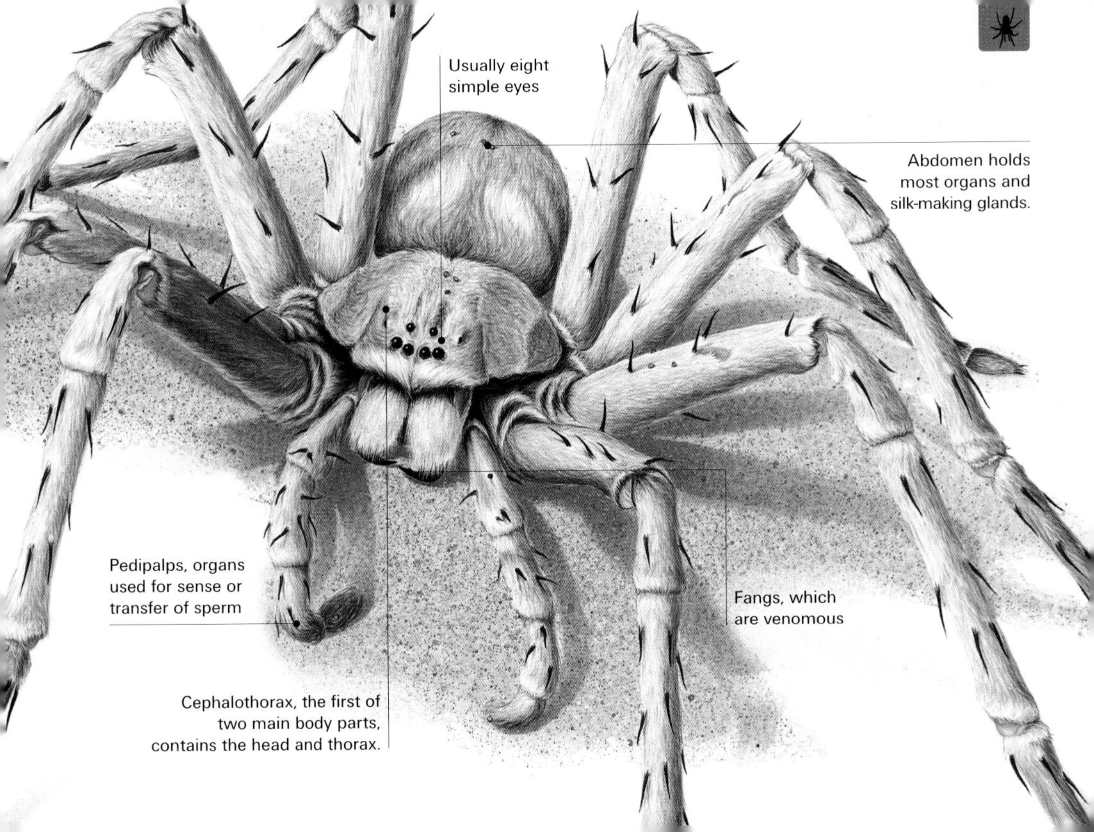

Usually eight
simple eyes

Abdomen holds
most organs and
silk-making glands.

Pedipalps, organs
used for sense or
transfer of sperm

Fangs, which
are venomous

Cephalothorax, the first of
two main body parts,
contains the head and thorax.

Other Arthropods

The word arthropod means "jointed foot." Arthropods make up more than 80 percent of all known animal species. They all have an exoskeleton of plates that meet at flexible joints. Muscles attach to the inside of these plates to make the body move. Different arthropods can be found on land, in the air, in fresh water, and in the oceans.

SHRIMP

Shrimps have two pairs of antennae and many pairs of limbs. These are for swimming, walking, or as claws.

CENTIPEDE
Centipedes and millipedes have long, segmented bodies, simple eyes, and many pairs of limbs.

CRAB

The front pair of a crab's ten pairs of legs are claws called chelipeds. They have two pairs of antennae.

PROTURAN

Proturans are tiny insect relatives that use the first of their three pairs of limbs to sense their surroundings.

HORSESHOE CRAB

With four pairs of limbs and pedipalps, horseshoe crabs are closely related to arachnids.

Classifying Insects

Insects are the largest group of arthropods. They are common both on land and in fresh water, but rarely live in the oceans and seas. This tree shows the evolution of modern insects from a possible common ancestor early in the Carboniferous period, more than 300 million years ago. Many insects, like dragonflies, have changed little over millions of years.

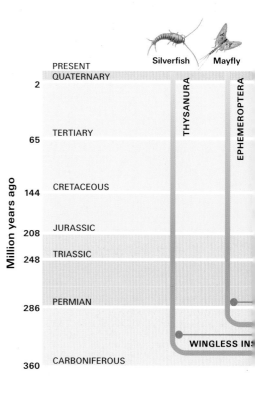

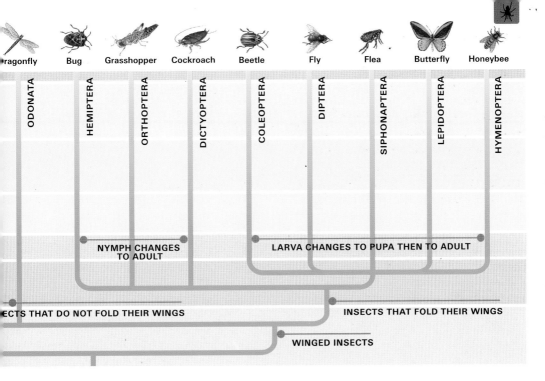

Dragonfly Bug Grasshopper Cockroach Beetle Fly Flea Butterfly Honeybee

ODONATA HEMIPTERA ORTHOPTERA DICTYOPTERA COLEOPTERA DIPTERA SIPHONAPTERA LEPIDOPTERA HYMENOPTERA

NYMPH CHANGES TO ADULT

LARVA CHANGES TO PUPA THEN TO ADULT

INSECTS THAT DO NOT FOLD THEIR WINGS

INSECTS THAT FOLD THEIR WINGS

WINGED INSECTS

Classifying Spiders

Arachnids include some of the most feared invertebrates. Aside from some aquatic mites and some water spiders, all arachnids live on land. This tree shows the evolution of modern arachnids from a possible common ancestor early in the Silurian period, more than 400 million years ago. While some spiders evolved recently, many arachnids are very similar to their ancient ancestors.

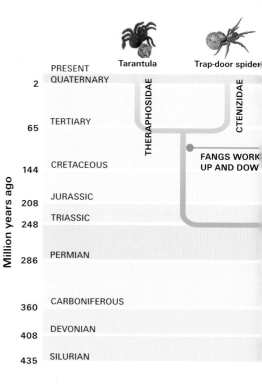

Tarantula

Trap-door spider

Million years ago		
PRESENT	THERAPHOSIDAE	CTENIZIDAE
2 QUATERNARY		
65 TERTIARY		
144 CRETACEOUS		FANGS WORK UP AND DOW
208 JURASSIC		
248 TRIASSIC		
286 PERMIAN		
360 CARBONIFEROUS		
408 DEVONIAN		
435 SILURIAN		

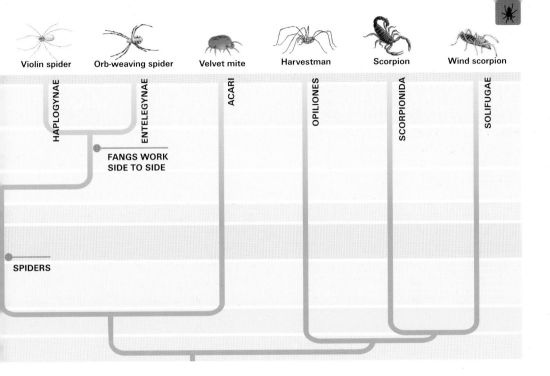

Violin spider Orb-weaving spider Velvet mite Harvestman Scorpion Wind scorpion

HAPLOGYNAE

ENTELEGYNAE

ACARI

OPILIONES

SCORPIONIDA

SOLIFUGAE

FANGS WORK
SIDE TO SIDE

SPIDERS

Beginnings

Earth formed 4,600 million years ago, and the first simple-celled organisms evolved millions of years later. However, it was in the Cambrian period that animal life exploded in diversity. Many marine arthropods became extinct, letting crustaceans dominate in the sea. Arthropods evolved onto land as insects and spiders.

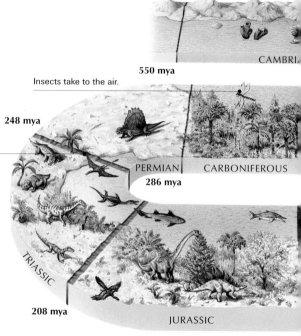

550 mya

CAMBRI

Insects take to the air.

248 mya

Trilobites and other marine arthropods become extinct.

PERMIAN | CARBONIFEROUS

286 mya

TRIASSIC

208 mya

JURASSIC

144 mya

KEY

Paleozoic era

Mesozoic era

Cenozoic era

Mass extinction

mya million years ago

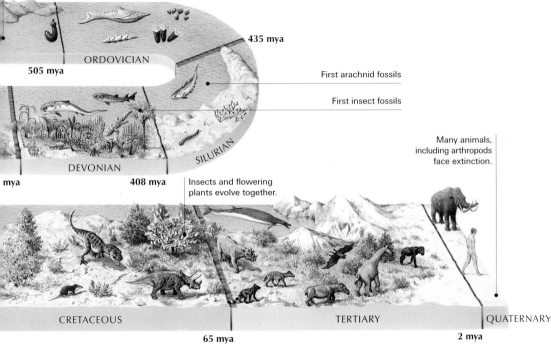

Trilobites rule the sea.

435 mya

ORDOVICIAN

505 mya

First arachnid fossils

First insect fossils

Many animals,
including arthropods
face extinction.

DEVONIAN

SILURIAN

mya

408 mya

Insects and flowering
plants evolve together.

CRETACEOUS

TERTIARY

QUATERNARY

65 mya

2 mya

21

Reading the Past

Even though they were common, early arthropods rarely became fossils because of their small size and delicate bodies. Fossils show that land-based insects and spiders were flourishing when vertebrates began to adapt to land. Insects may have evolved from ancient centipede-like ancestors. The earliest fossil arachnids, ancient scorpions, are estimated to be 425 million years old.

HORSESHOE CRAB
Horseshoe crabs have changed little in 200 million years.

DRAGONFLY

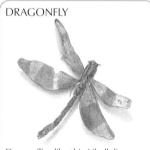

Dragonflies like this *Libellulium* sp. lived about 200 million years ago.

TRILOBITE

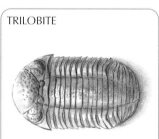

Trilobites were common from 500 to 250 million years ago.

SNAKEFLY

Snakefly fossils have been found dating from 250 million years ago.

PRECIOUS FOSSILS

Amber, or fossilized tree sap, contains the best examples of ancient insects and spiders. Insect hairs, and even DNA fragments, can be preserved.

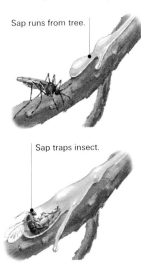

Sap runs from tree.

Sap traps insect.

Small World

Bugs' bodies need to be light, or they would be too heavy to move or especially to fly. Bugs have turned being small into an advantage by using spaces that are too cramped for other animals. These include the space between the upper and lower surfaces of leaves, and between grains of soil. Because they are so small, individuals need very little food.

WINGS FOR FLYING
Insects are small, so their papery wings can lift them into the air.

WALL CLIMBERS

Flies are so light that small suckers are all they need to climb up walls and walk on the ceiling.

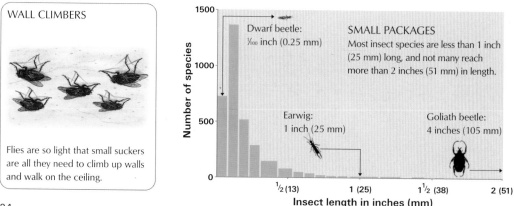

Dwarf beetle:
¹/₁₀₀ inch (0.25 mm)

SMALL PACKAGES
Most insect species are less than 1 inch (25 mm) long, and not many reach more than 2 inches (51 mm) in length.

Earwig:
1 inch (25 mm)

Goliath beetle:
4 inches (105 mm)

Number of species

1500
1000
500
0

¹/₂ (13)   1 (25)   1¹/₂ (38)   2 (51)
Insect length in inches (mm)

Under the Microscope

Some bugs are so small they can be seen only under a microscope. Others can be seen with the naked eye, but a microscope is needed to study their features.

MINI MITES
Like most species of mites, this one can be seen only under a microscope.

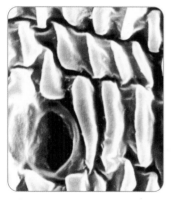

HOLE STORY
Tiny airholes, called spiracles, in an insect's exoskeleton allow it to breathe.

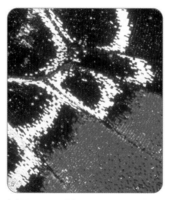

SCALY WINGS
The wings of butterflies and moths are covered in tiny, overlapping scales.

JAWS FOR CHEWING
A grasshopper's mouth is well adapted for grasping and chewing plants.

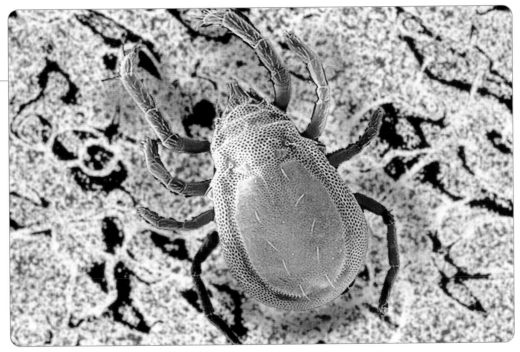

Outside an Insect

With large eyes, razor-sharp jaws, and powerful running legs, this tiger beetle deserves its name. Its eyes can detect the smallest movements of a potential victim. Its legs can carry it at speeds that outrun most other insects.

A beetle has elytra, or wing cases, that protect the delicate flying wings.

The abdomen contains most of the vital organs.

DID YOU KNOW?

An insect's foot may have hooks, pads, or suckers to help it hold on.

Most insects have six legs, which are usually divided into five parts.

The legs and wings are attached to the thorax.

The head is one of the strongest body parts.

An insect's antennae can detect chemicals, heat, and vibrations.

The jaws, or mandibles, of this insect are tough, sharp, and powerful.

Each of this beetle's compound eyes has 26,000 lenses.

These palps are sense organs that taste and guide food to the mouth.

Inside an Insect

With its external skeleton cut away, this wasp's organs are revealed in color code. The breathing system is light blue. The system for digesting food is green. The blood circulation system is red, and the central nervous system is dark blue.

Reproductive organs

HOW INSECTS BREATHE

Spiracle (airhole)

Trachea

Air is taken directly to tissue through tracheae.

Balloon-like air sacs act like bellows to draw air in and out.

Food goes through the midgut as it is digested.

Ganglia are little brains that help control the organs.

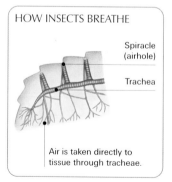

The tubelike heart
pumps blood
around the body.

The brain coordinates
most muscles and the
insect's behavior.

Delicate hairs detect
movement, temperature,
and chemicals.

31

Outside a Spider

This marbled orb weaver is not a danger to humans. In fact, it is a big help. It will eat more than 350 insects in its lifetime. Despite their bad reputation, spiders are natural pest controllers, helping to limit populations of cockroaches, flies, and locusts.

Many spiders have toothed claws, plus hairs that help them grip their webs.

UNDERNEATH A SPIDER

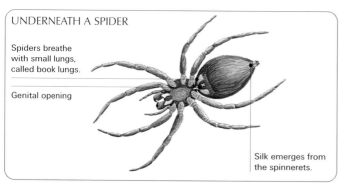

Spiders breathe with small lungs, called book lungs.

Genital opening

Silk emerges from the spinnerets.

All spiders have eight jointed legs.

Two fangs with venom ducts

The abdomen contains the silk-making glands and most organs.

Some spiders have excellent eyesight. Others are blind.

Spiders use pedipalps as sense organs or to transfer sperm.

The legs and jaws attach to the cephalothorax.

Cephalothorax includes the head and thorax.

Spider's heart runs along the top of the abdomen.

Food is broken down in the midgut, then into the bloodstream.

The female's eggs are produced in the ovaries.

The spinnerets weave silk.

Food is drawn into the sucking stomach.

Oxygen enters through the book lung.

The silk gland produces liquid silk.

Glands on the base of the fangs produce venom.

Inside a Spider

To get a clearer idea of how a spider functions, take a look inside the body of a brown badge huntsman.

The brain coordinates body function.

Growing and Molting

Aside from the joints, the exoskeleton is hard and inflexible, and does not allow a bug to grow. Bugs shed their old exoskeleton and replace it with a new, larger one at regular intervals. This allows them to grow to adult size and shape. Some bugs molt only twice in their lifetime, but others molt more than 25 times.

JUST-MOLTED MANTIS
This mantis has just molted. Antennae can still be seen on its old exoskeleton.

READY TO MOLT

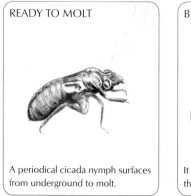

A periodical cicada nymph surfaces from underground to molt.

BREAKING OUT

It emerges from its old exoskeleton through a split in the thorax.

WAITING TO DRY

After it has broken free, the cicada needs to wait for its skin to harden.

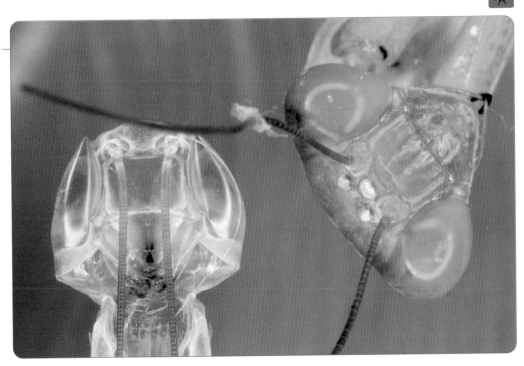

Spider Molt

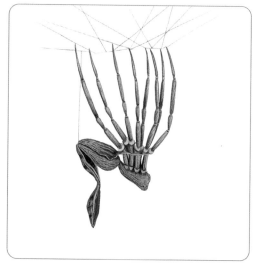

SPLIT START

A female giant wood spider hangs from her web as her old exoskeleton splits along the edge of her cephalothorax. Female spiders continue to molt even after adulthood.

BIG BREAK

Her exoskeleton tears apart and starts to come away as she tries to pull her legs free. The conditions have to be right—if the weather is too dry, she could get stuck and die.

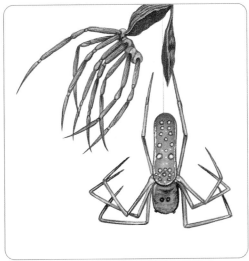

LEGS OUT

The spider pulls her long, fragile legs clear of the old skin very slowly. It is like taking off a glove, but if anything goes wrong, she could end up without her new legs.

FREE DANGLE

Finally free, the spider dangles by a silk thread from the old exoskeleton as blood pumps around her new body. This expands her new exoskeleton while it is still soft.

Insect Senses

To survive, an insect must be able to find food, track down a mate, and, most important of all, detect its enemies before they have a chance to attack. Like many other animals, insects have five main senses—sight, hearing, smell, touch, and taste. Different insects use some of these senses more than others.

Small eyes on the top of the head, known as ocelli, sense the difference between light and shade.

Compound eyes contain thousands of lenses. Each of these transmits a different part of an image.

Heat-sensitive antennae are used to locate exposed areas of skin.

FEELING ITS WAY
Caterpillars like this one rely on body hairs to sense their environment.

HORSING AROUND
Female horseflies feed on blood, and rely mainly on vision to track down a meal.

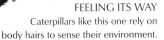

Antennae

Insects use antennae to smell, touch, and hear. The shape of antennae varies among insects, and sometimes even between males and females of the same species. Antennae help insects to find a mate, feel the air, or find the best place to feed.

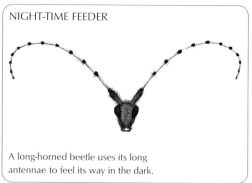

MATE SEEKER
In flight, a male cockchafer's antennae open out to detect the scent of a mate.

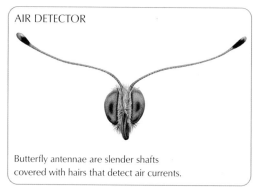

AIR DETECTOR

Butterfly antennae are slender shafts covered with hairs that detect air currents.

NIGHT-TIME FEEDER

A long-horned beetle uses its long antennae to feel its way in the dark.

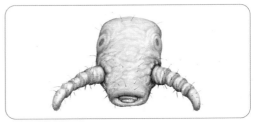

DAMP SPOT SEARCHER
A human louse uses its antennae to sense damp parts of the body, where it feeds on blood.

FEATHERY SNIFFER

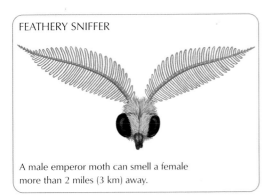

A male emperor moth can smell a female more than 2 miles (3 km) away.

HOT SPOT HUNTER

A female mosquito's feathery antennae sense heat from warm-blooded animals.

On the Scent

Ants use their antennae to sniff out food and leave a scent to show other ants where the food source is. Butterflies, however, use more than the antennae on their heads to find food. Butterflies have sense organs on their feet that let them know when they land on something good to eat.

TASTY LANDING
After landing on a flower, a butterfly will check the taste with its feet.

TAILORED SCENTS
Tailor ants like this pair use their antennae to detect the scent of their colony's territory.

FOOD CONFUSION

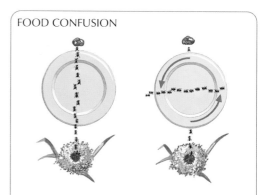

If you rotate a plate with a trail of ants on it by 90 degrees, the ants will lose their way to the food source.

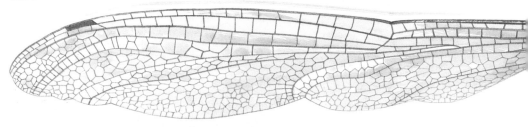

Ways of Seeing

The green darner dragonfly's eyes have 28,000 lenses each. The dragonfly can see in every direction at once. Even at dusk, it can pluck a darting mosquito from the air.

HUMAN AND INSECT VIEWS
Many insects have eyes that are sensitive to ultraviolet light, so they see shapes and patterns that are invisible to us.

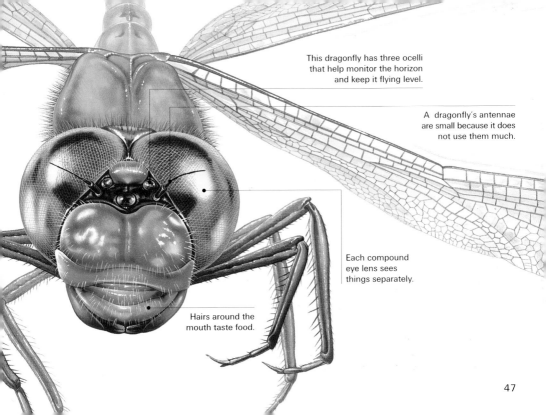

This dragonfly has three ocelli that help monitor the horizon and keep it flying level.

A dragonfly's antennae are small because it does not use them much.

Each compound eye lens sees things separately.

Hairs around the mouth taste food.

47

Detecting Sound

An insect's sense organs are scattered throughout its body. Insects often use their antennae to hear, but they also have other ways of detecting sounds and vibrations. Some have thin membranes called tympanum, much like human eardrums, on their thorax, abdomen, or even on their legs. Others sense vibration and movement through their legs or wings.

HEARING THE CALL
Grasshoppers are particularly sensitive to calls made by their own species.

EARS ON FRONT LEGS

A bush cricket's ear is a thin oval membrane that senses vibrations.

GUT FEELING

Grasshoppers detect sound through tympanum on their abdomen.

LEG BRISTLES

A cockroach uses leg bristles to sense something coming toward it.

EARS ON THE THORAX

Some butterflies have tympanum on their thorax that detect sound.

FEELING THE GROUND

Ants sense vibrations through their legs, often responding by attack.

WINGS AS EARS

The delicate wings of a lacewing sense movement and vibration.

Spider Senses

Spiders have a number of eyes—one pair forms images and smaller eyes detect movement. Most spiders have poor eyesight, but some hunting spiders have sharp vision. They use fine hairs on their body and legs to find prey and to avoid danger. Slits in the exoskeleton may detect odors, gravity, or vibrations.

FROM LEAF TO LEAF
Plexippus jumping spiders have sharp eyesight that accurately judges the distance between leaves.

TRAPPED IN THE WEB
A spider's leg hairs sense when prey get entangled.

DID YOU KNOW?
Special hollow hairs on the pedipalps and legs allow most spiders to smell.

Detecting Signals

Many spiders rely on sensitive body hairs to detect vibrations and sense movement. Each hair is anchored in a tiny pit surrounded by nerve endings. A vibration from any direction will move the hair. Web-spinning spiders use these organs to sense if prey is trapped in their webs. Hunting spiders quickly respond to vibrations when searching for prey.

LEGGY PREDATOR
The hairs on the legs and body of this spider can easily be seen.

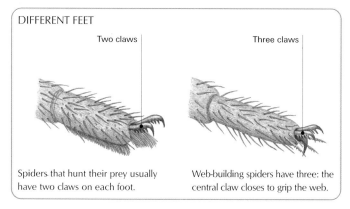

DIFFERENT FEET

Two claws

Three claws

Spiders that hunt their prey usually have two claws on each foot.

Web-building spiders have three: the central claw closes to grip the web.

A CLOSER VIEW
Spider hairs seen through a microscope

Spider Eyes

CRAB SPIDER

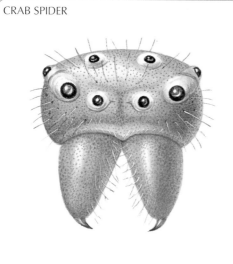

The crab spider's vibration sensors help it to detect possible prey from a distance. Its sharp vision picks up the prey as it draws in closer to its hiding spot.

WOODLOUSE-EATING SPIDER

The woodlouse-eating spider has six very small eyes. It uses its sense of touch, rather than its weak eyesight, to uncover prey under stones and bark.

OGRE-FACED SPIDER

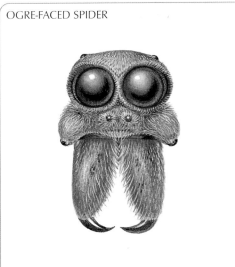

The ogre-faced spider has two huge eyes that are hundreds of times more sensitive to light than human eyes. It can see prey in near-total darkness.

HUNTSMAN SPIDER

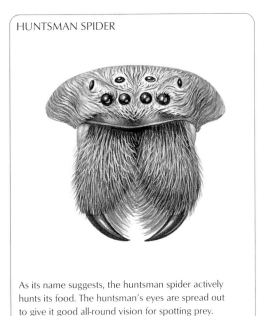

As its name suggests, the huntsman spider actively hunts its food. The huntsman's eyes are spread out to give it good all-round vision for spotting prey.

CALLING OUT
Grasshoppers call by rubbing their legs against their wings.

Bug Communication

Insects and spiders communicate in different ways. Some use scent signals. Many communicate with light, dance, or color. Others make their own special sound. Some of these sounds are familiar, like the chirp of crickets, or the drone of cicadas.

LISTEN CLOSELY
A microscope shows the sound organ (tympanum) of a grasshopper. These receptors relay vibrations to the brain.

THE LOUDEST INSECT

Mating mole crickets are so noisy they can be heard half a mile (800 m) away.

Communicating in the Hive

Honeybees live in a complex society. There can be more than 60,000 bees in a hive, so they need to stay in contact with each other to keep the hive in order. They dance to tell other bees where they have found nectar or pollen.

ALL ABUZZ IN THE HIVE
These bees work together to make the wax cells that store honey.

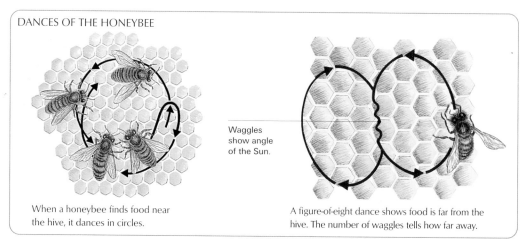

DANCES OF THE HONEYBEE

Waggles show angle of the Sun.

When a honeybee finds food near the hive, it dances in circles.

A figure-of-eight dance shows food is far from the hive. The number of waggles tells how far away.

Lights in the Night

Fireflies are not flies at all; they are actually small beetles. After dark, they use their flashing light organs to find a mate. The males flash as they fly overhead and females flash from the ground.

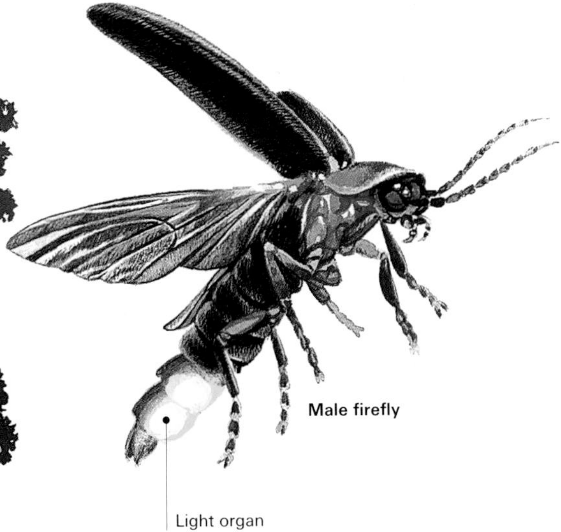

Male firefly

Light organ

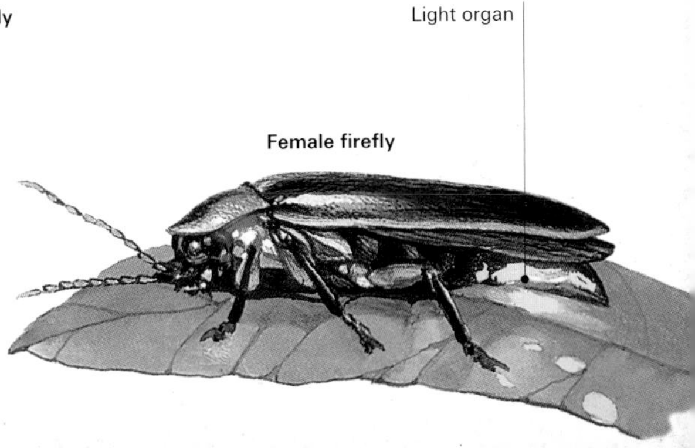

Light organ

Female firefly

DANCING LIGHTS
Each species of firefly flashes in its own distinct pattern. This is to make sure the female attracts the same species of male.

Tapping Messages

Many insects and spiders make vibrations to send each other messages. They tap messages to warn others of danger, to attract a mate, or to identify themselves. They use touch to recognize other members of their colony.

HEAD BANGER

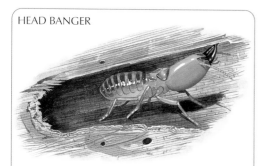

Termites live in underground nests. When something threatens their nest, they bang their heads against the tunnel walls. The vibration alerts others to the danger.

TUNING IN

The tiny male signature spider needs to let the female know he is not her dinner. He plucks the web using a special code, known only to their species.

RIPPLES ACROSS THE WATER
When a male raft spider wants to mate, he sends a message of ripples to a female. She senses the pattern with her feet.

TOUCHY FEELY
Ants recognize each other by smell. Two ants gently touch their antennae together, testing their scents to see if they are from the same nest.

63

Spider Communication

Some male spiders dance to impress a female. Other spiders, even with all their eyes, do not see well. To contact a new mate, they might use tapping signals on their webs or on the ground that are unique to their species.

JUMPING SPIDERS
This male jumping spider waves his front legs to show off his colors and patterns to the female to show he is a possible mate.

BUG BEHAVIOR

On the Wing

Insects were the first animals to fly. They
do some amazing things with their wings:
painted lady butterflies set out from North
Africa and can reach the Arctic Circle—a
distance of more than 1,800 miles (2,900 km).

Taking Off

Flying insects take off in many ways. Butterflies start with their wings held together above their back. They then lower them rapidly, and the air draft sucks them upward. Weak flyers jump off a high point like the stem of a plant to help them get airborne.

GETTING READY
The front wings open so the back wings can start to unfold.

Front wings closed

GROUNDED LADYBUG
This beetle's hard front wings cover the soft flying wings underneath.

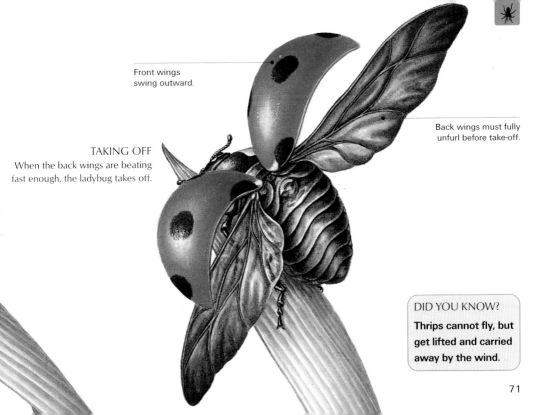

Front wings
swing outward.

Back wings must fully
unfurl before take-off.

TAKING OFF
When the back wings are beating
fast enough, the ladybug takes off.

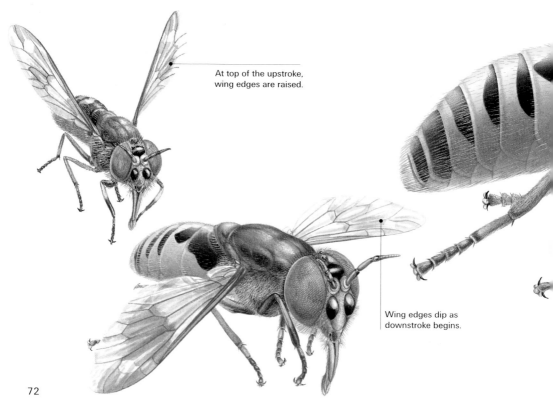

At top of the upstroke, wing edges are raised.

Wing edges dip as downstroke begins.

72

How Wings Work

Most insects have one or two pairs of wings. Bees, wasps, butterflies, and dragonflies use both pairs for flying, but beetles use only one pair. Strong muscles power all wings. A midge beats its wings around 1,000 times a second. Hoverflies can zoom, hover, or change direction extremely fast.

TILT AND FLAP
A deerfly tilts its wings as they flap to get the thrust to take off or to fly faster.

The greater the angle, the stronger the thrust

73

Comparing Wings

Insects started working out how to fly about 270 million years ago. Since then, they have become incredibly good at finding new ways to fly. There are many different types of wings and they do many different types of things. Some are for gliding, others are for acrobatics. Some are for flying long distances, and others are for speedy escapes.

FLIES

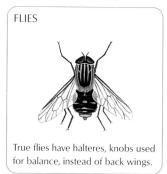

True flies have halteres, knobs used for balance, instead of back wings.

THRIPS

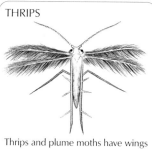

Thrips and plume moths have wings that look like small feathers.

WASPS

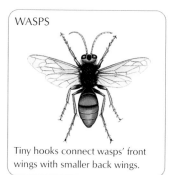

Tiny hooks connect wasps' front wings with smaller back wings.

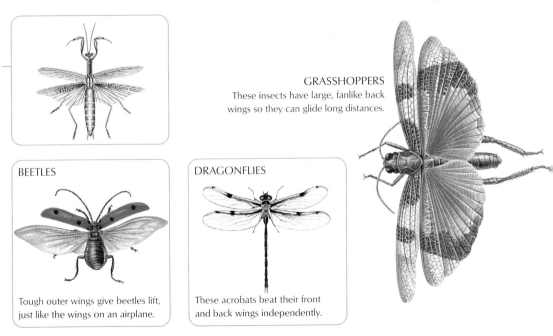

GRASSHOPPERS
These insects have large, fanlike back wings so they can glide long distances.

BEETLES
Tough outer wings give beetles lift, just like the wings on an airplane.

DRAGONFLIES
These acrobats beat their front and back wings independently.

Flying Fast, Flying Far

Most insects have wings but not all of them can fly fast. Some slow flyers, like butterflies, can travel long distances. Two-winged flyers such as flies are superfast, which is why they can be so hard to swat.

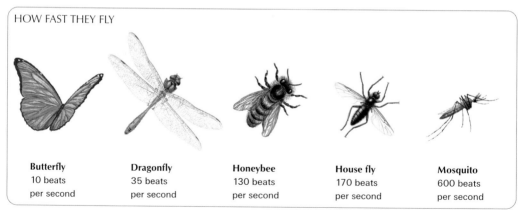

HOW FAST THEY FLY

Butterfly
10 beats
per second

Dragonfly
35 beats
per second

Honeybee
130 beats
per second

House fly
170 beats
per second

Mosquito
600 beats
per second

SPEEDING TICKET
Dragonflies are the fastest flying insects. They can fly 31 miles (50 km) per hour.

Excellent eyesight

Friction-reducing wings

Damselflies rest with their wings above their body.

Types of Legs

Adult insects have six legs with several joints; some juveniles have even more. This makes them very stable. Legs have equipment like hairs, spines, or suction pads that allow insects to hang upside down, jump, or swim. Some legs are so powerful their owners can jump many times their own body length.

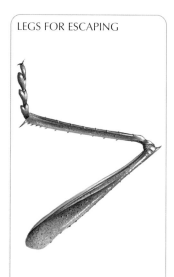

LEGS FOR ESCAPING

The back legs of crickets are long and bent back for jumping.

LEGS FOR GRASPING
Caterpillars have legs on their abdomen as well as on their thorax; these help their long bodies hang onto stems.

LEGS FOR HANGING ON

Flies' feet have suction pads to help them stick to smooth surfaces.

LEGS FOR HUNTING

Praying mantis' barbed front legs can grab prey at lightning speed.

LEGS FOR SWIMMING

Diving beetles have strong, hairy legs that they use like paddles.

Ways of Moving

The slowest insects are legless larvae, which wriggle to move about. The fastest are jumpers and flyers, like fleas and dragonflies. Swimmers such as water boatmen and diving beetles use their legs like oars.

THREE BY THREE
Insects walk three legs at a time, moving two legs on one side and one on the other.

CATERPILLAR LOOPING

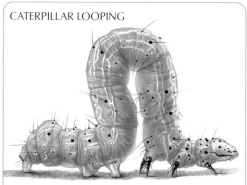

Holding on with its front legs, this caterpillar pulls its body into a loop, then stretches forward to straighten.

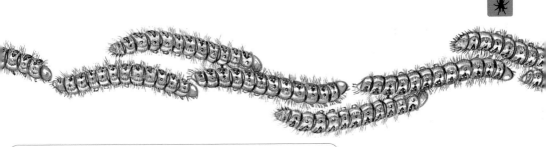

FLIPPING UP AND OVER

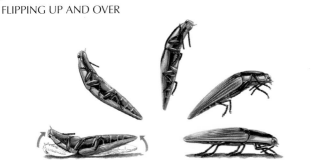

When a click beetle is disturbed, it lies very still on its back. If this does not work, it snaps its head and abdomen upward, which hurls the beetle into the air.

A HAIRY TRAIL

One by one, processionary caterpillars line up, traveling in long lines in search of soft soil to burrow into to pupate.

DID YOU KNOW?

Head lice grip so firmly that they can be removed only with a special comb.

A Great Spring

The back legs of some insects, like grasshoppers, are so powerful they can leap very swiftly. They flick their legs backward and launch themselves into the air. Strong muscles provide most of the power, but a springlike joint in the knees adds even more force.

Homes and Habitats

Bugs make their homes in almost every habitat on Earth. A habitat is a place where an animal lives, and includes the weather, plants, and other animal life. Bugs live in the driest deserts and the wettest rain forests; they live above ground, below ground, and in fresh water.

RAIN FOREST DESTROYED
Butterflies lose their habitat when forests are damaged by machinery.

SMELLY HIDEAWAY
Southern stink bugs like warm climates. They hide in tree bark or leaf litter over winter before emerging to lay eggs.

Deserts

Life can be a challenge in hot, dry places where water is scarce. Yet deserts are havens for many types of bugs. They have found ways to live in these harsh places. Many insects and spiders live underground to escape the intense rays of the Sun.

IN AMERICA'S DESERTS
Desert hairy scorpions escape the heat by sleeping all day under rocks.

IN AUSTRALIA'S RED CENTER
Honeypot ants store extra nectar in their bodies to feed the colony in dry periods.

IN AFRICA'S NAMIB DESERT

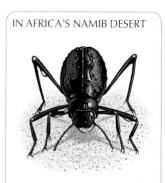

The darkling beetle collects mist from the ocean by pointing into the wind and collecting the "dew."

THE EATING MACHINE

Caterpillars are made to eat. They can grow 2,000 times the size of their eggs. So they need a lot of plants to feed on.

Woodlands and Rain Forests

Lush, moist, plant-filled forests teem with bug life. Rain forests have so many bugs that many are still unknown. Such habitats are millions of years old, so different species of insects and spiders have found their own place in the forest.

STRONG JAWS ARE FOR CHOMPING
Grasshoppers are hungry plant eaters. They are not always fussy but they need a lot of food, so forests are ideal.

Underwater

Creeks, ponds, and lakes teem with bug life. Some insects are light enough to float on or scamper over the surface; others have found ways of breathing underwater.

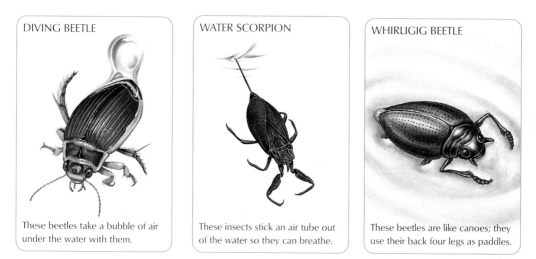

DIVING BEETLE

These beetles take a bubble of air under the water with them.

WATER SCORPION

These insects stick an air tube out of the water so they can breathe.

WHIRLIGIG BEETLE

These beetles are like canoes; they use their back four legs as paddles.

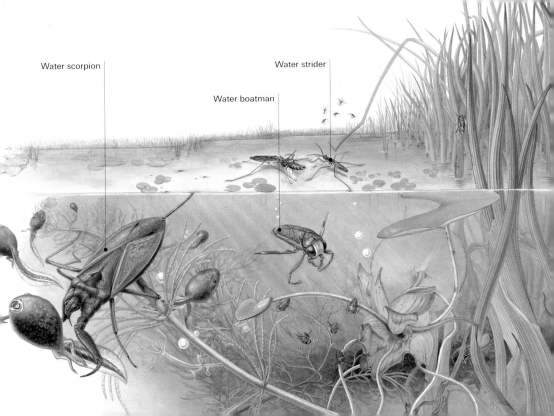

Water scorpion

Water strider

Water boatman

Underground

Beneath the soil and burrowing deep down are many creatures living underground. There are spiders in burrows, ants in nests, and cicada nymphs sucking on tree roots. Underground dwellers need to stop predators from getting in: some use trap doors, others build fortresses.

Hiding place

Trap-door spider

SECRET CHAMBER
This trap-door spider hides from predators in a chamber. It has a special door it can pull shut.

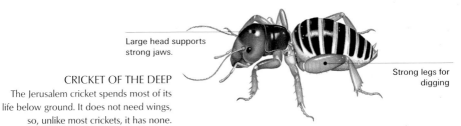

Large head supports strong jaws.

Strong legs for digging

CRICKET OF THE DEEP

The Jerusalem cricket spends most of its life below ground. It does not need wings, so, unlike most crickets, it has none.

DIPLURAN

Diplurans are closely related to insects. They are usually found pushing their way through soil and rotting leaf litter.

SPRINGTAILS

These small insect relatives are named because they can leap to amazing heights. Most live in soil, leaf litter, or bark.

Living on Others

Some insects and spiders fall victim to parasites. These are animals that live by feeding on others, usually inside them. Some wasps lay their eggs in host insects or spiders. Tiny mites attack bugs, too.

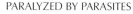

UNWANTED GUEST
This flea lives among the feathers of a house martin. It lays its eggs in the bird's nest so that fleas will infect the chicks.

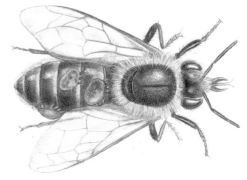

DEADLY MITES
Varroa mites can kill an entire honeybee colony. The mites get inside the bees' bodies in between the segments.

Nests and Shelters

To shelter from the elements as well as their enemies, insects and spiders protect themselves in nests, webs, and other shelters. The nests of ants, termites, wasps, and bees are often elaborate structures, suitable for colonies of many thousands of individuals. During metamorphosis, the pupae of some insects protect themselves in cases.

SEETHING SWARM
Processionary caterpillars build weblike nests and live in huddled groups.

SLEEPING BAGS

These cases are homes for bagworm caterpillars. Different species use different materials and create different shapes.

THE CHRYSALIS
The adult monarch butterfly is almost ready to emerge from its pupal case.

Wasp World

A single queen common wasp starts building the nest. Using chewed wood fibers, she builds a hanging cup. Then she adds a series of cells and lays worker-wasp eggs in them. Some extra layers are added to keep them warm. When they grow up, these worker wasps take over the task of expanding the nest. They tear down the old walls and build new layers.

PAPER WASPS AS INVENTORS
These delicate nests inspired China's Ts'ai Lun (AD 89–106) to invent paper.

HOW TO BUILD A WASP NEST

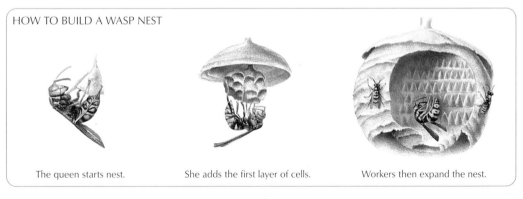

The queen starts nest.

She adds the first layer of cells.

Workers then expand the nest.

Termite Tunnels and Towers

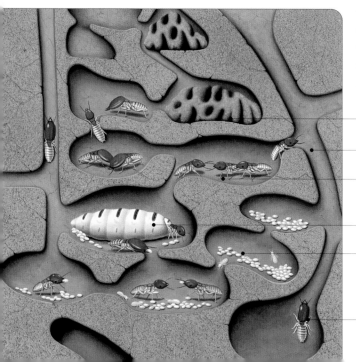

Termites live in large colonies where some chambers are used to farm fungus for food. A termite queen can live for 15 years and lay up to 14 million eggs.

Fungus combs

Ventilation shaft

Workers' chamber

Queen's chamber

Nursery with eggs and nymphs

Soldier termite

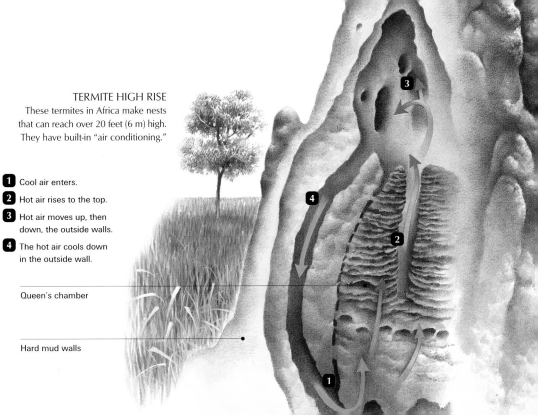

TERMITE HIGH RISE
These termites in Africa make nests that can reach over 20 feet (6 m) high. They have built-in "air conditioning."

1 Cool air enters.

2 Hot air rises to the top.

3 Hot air moves up, then down, the outside walls.

4 The hot air cools down in the outside wall.

Queen's chamber

Hard mud walls

Building with Leaves

Leaves make great homes. Leaf-cutter bees clip off bits of leaf to make tube-shaped cells for their larvae. Some spiders shelter in a curled leaf they fasten with silk. Froghoppers live on leaves by burying themselves in froth.

WEAVING A WALL
Weaver ants link together in a grid of "ant scaffolding" to build their nest.

IN THE SHELTER OF A LEAF
Paper wasps build their nests under shelter, such as under a leaf, a tree trunk, or even under the overhang of a building.

SEWING UP THE WALLS
These green tree ants act like clips, holding two leaves together. Others will come and sew them up with silk.

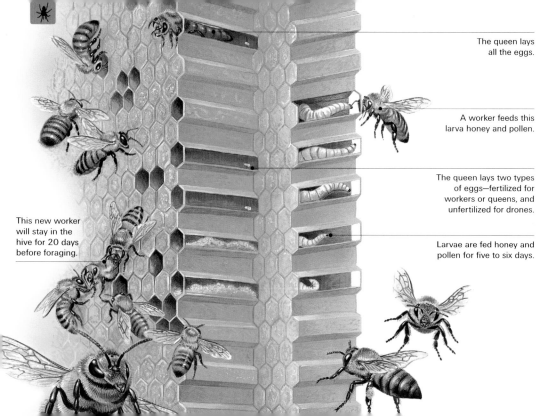

The queen lays all the eggs.

A worker feeds this larva honey and pollen.

The queen lays two types of eggs—fertilized for workers or queens, and unfertilized for drones.

Larvae are fed honey and pollen for five to six days.

This new worker will stay in the hive for 20 days before foraging.

Beehives

This complex nest can house up to 60,000 bees. Hive work is divided among three groups: the queen bee, who controls the hive; the male drones, who mate with the queen; and the female workers.

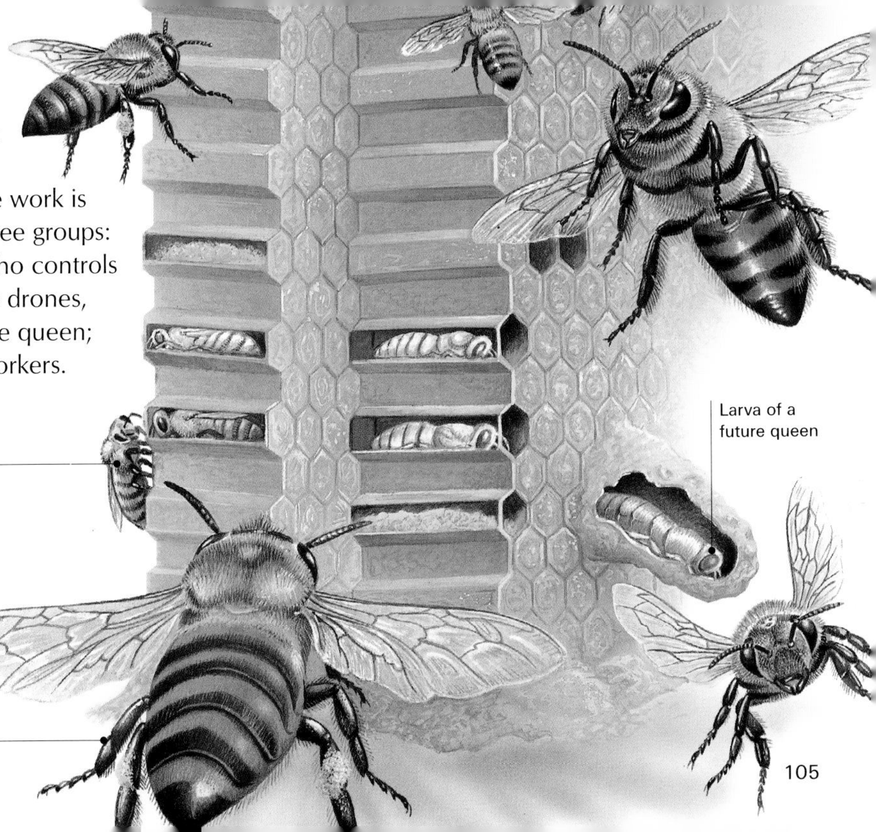

A worker bee places a wax seal to cap the cell of a mature larva.

A worker bee returns with pollen.

Larva of a future queen

Ant Nests

Ants are social insects that work together for the survival of the colony. Colonies can range from a few dozen ants to more than 300 million. Most ants build their nests either above or below ground in the soil, in wood, or on plants.

QUEEN

The queen ant's job is to lay all the eggs in the colony.

THE ANTS COME MARCHING
Matabele ants of Africa swarm in thousands to raid termite nests. They follow a scent trail to the nest.

MALE

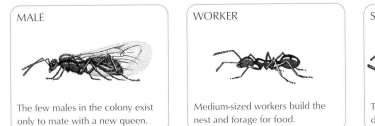

The few males in the colony exist only to mate with a new queen.

WORKER

Medium-sized workers build the nest and forage for food.

SOLDIER

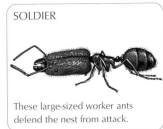

These large-sized worker ants defend the nest from attack.

A Portable Home

Some insect larvae build portable cases using twigs, reeds, sand, tiny stones, and even snail shells to protect themselves. Some, such as those of caddisflies and case moths, have elaborate designs. Some wasps lay their eggs on or inside a spider or caterpillar, giving their young a "lunch on legs."

CADDISFLY LARVA
The larva of the blackfly hunter (left) builds a case from sand, sticks, or leaves to protect itself. It will emerge as an adult (right).

UNDERWATER CASE
Caddisfly larvae feed by extending their head out from their case.

DID YOU KNOW?

Caddisfly larvae can make cases out of anything, even jewels, if they are close by.

READY-MADE MEAL
A parasitic wasp has laid its eggs on a hairy caterpillar. The unlucky caterpillar will become the first meal for the wasp larvae inside.

Silks and Webs

Spiders make up to seven different kinds of silk. They pull strands of silk from finger-like projections called spinnerets. These work the silk into different forms to build webs, traplines or draglines, to line burrows, or to wrap prey or eggs.

CASE BY CASE
Many spiders make a case out of silk to store and protect their eggs.

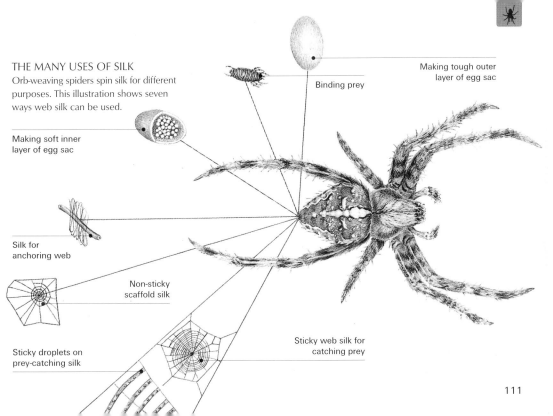

THE MANY USES OF SILK

Orb-weaving spiders spin silk for different purposes. This illustration shows seven ways web silk can be used.

Making tough outer layer of egg sac

Binding prey

Making soft inner layer of egg sac

Silk for anchoring web

Non-sticky scaffold silk

Sticky droplets on prey-catching silk

Sticky web silk for catching prey

The Webs They Weave

A spider web's scaffolding is made from dry silk, which the spider can walk on without getting stuck. A layer of sticky silk is added to trap any insects that fly into it.

ATTRACTIVE TRAP
Some spiders decorate their webs with special silk that may attract prey to the web.

SCAFFOLD WEB
Sticky silk threads stretch from the web to the ground. They snap back into the air when touched by any insect prey.

HOW TO BUILD AN ORB WEB
The spider lets out a single strand of silk. When it connects to a branch, the spider then builds the first fork of the web.

The fork is anchored and the frame is built. Scaffold threads are attached. Then a spiral of sticky silk is added.

Kinds of Webs

DEW-COVERED ORB WEB
Spider webs can get covered with early morning dew. Many spiders build webs facing the Sun so their web dries faster.

Some spiders build the familiar circular orb webs often seen in gardens. Others make two-tiered webs covering low bushes, or webs shaped like hammocks, sheets, or triangles. Some are tidy; others look like a tangled mess. Some spiders build a new web every night. Others make repairs when needed.

ORB WEB

Orb webs are circular and have a spiral of sticky threads.

HAMMOCK WEB

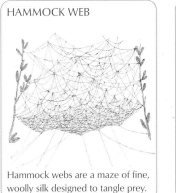

Hammock webs are a maze of fine, woolly silk designed to tangle prey.

TRIANGLE WEB

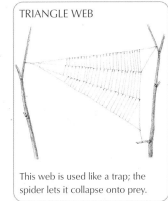

This web is used like a trap; the spider lets it collapse onto prey.

115

Funnels and Trap Doors

Some spiders build their webs in the ground. These have
a small opening, such as a funnel or a door. The spider lives
in a burrow below, waiting to pounce on any unwary prey.

TRAP DOOR
These spiders hide their
burrows with a door.

FUNNEL WEAVER
This spider's web has a funnel where it sits and waits to trap prey.

Snaring and Wrapping Prey

Spiders use some amazing ways to catch their prey. Some lasso their prey with a silk thread or net. Almost all spiders inject their prey with venom to stun it. There are also pirate spiders. They throw a line to another spider's web to feel the tug when a meal is caught—then they steal it.

STUNNED PREY
After injecting its prey with venom, the spider wraps it.

IN THE LAIR OF A PURSE SPIDER

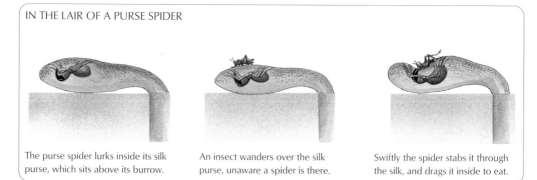

The purse spider lurks inside its silk purse, which sits above its burrow.

An insect wanders over the silk purse, unaware a spider is there.

Swiftly the spider stabs it through the silk, and drags it inside to eat.

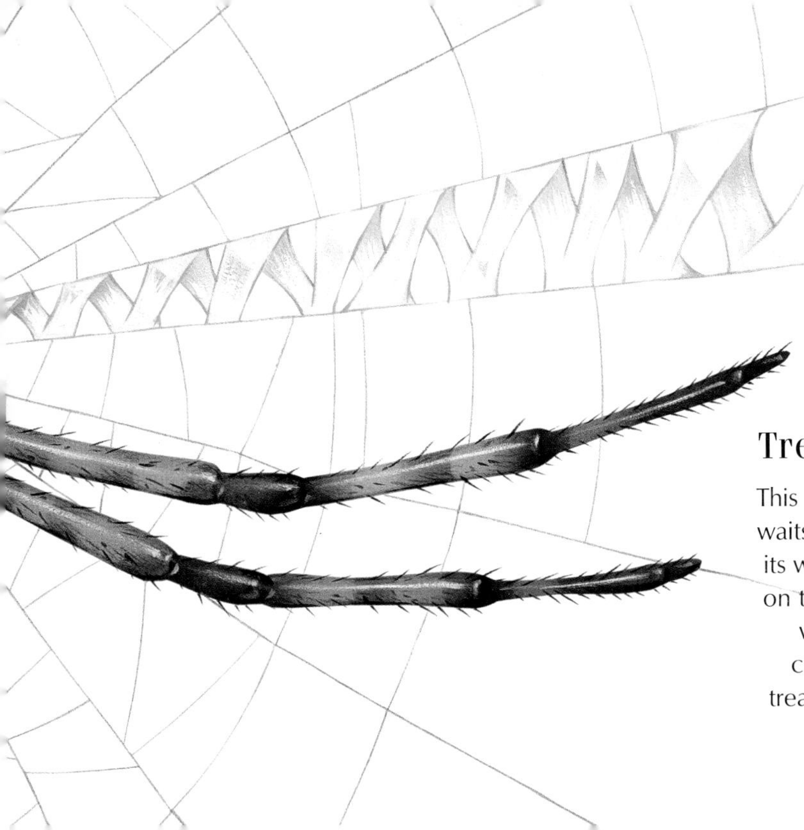

Treading Lightly

This African signature spider waits for an insect to fly into its web. The prey gets stuck on the sticky threads in the web, which the spider is careful not to walk on. It treads only on the nonstick scaffold of the web.

Draglines and Threads

Jumping, flying, and trickery are also possible with silk. Bolas spiders twirl out a thread of silk, which has sticky droplets at the end. A scent in these droplets attracts male moths that think there is a mate nearby.

LEAPING TO LUNCH
A jumping spider sends out a silk dragline as it jumps onto its prey.

BALLOONING
Spiders can squeeze out silk to catch the wind and float away.

HOW TO CATCH A MOTH

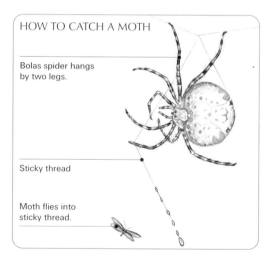

Bolas spider hangs by two legs.

Sticky thread

Moth flies into sticky thread.

STAYING ALIVE

Attack and Defense

Insects are always being attacked by mammals, birds, lizards, spiders, and other insects. Many defend themselves by retreating or hiding. Others use bright colors as a warning that they are dangerous themselves. Some harmless insects imitate the colors of those that are poisonous. Many insect and spider predators use a number of similar tricks and tactics to catch their prey.

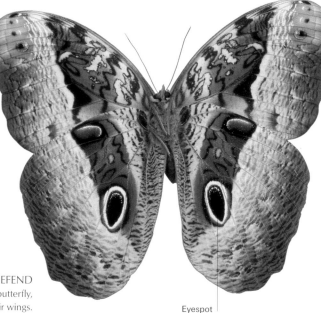

EYES TO DEFEND
Many moths and butterflies, like this owl butterfly, have large eyespots underneath their wings.

Eyespot

ON THE ATTACK
The bright green color of this praying mantis blends with
the surrounding leaves as it waits by flowers for prey.

Warning Signs

While bugs are small, they have many ways to defend themselves. Wasps and bees have poisonous stings; others, like ants and beetles, bite. Spiders and scorpions inject their enemies with poison from fangs or stings in their tails.

KICKING BACK

Known by the New Zealand Maori as "the god of ugly things," giant weta are ancient crickets. They throw their sharply spined legs into the air in warning, but rarely bite.

RAISING THE ALARM

The Australian funnel-web spider is aggressive if its territory is threatened. It rears up on its back legs to expose its fangs, which inject a poison that can be deadly.

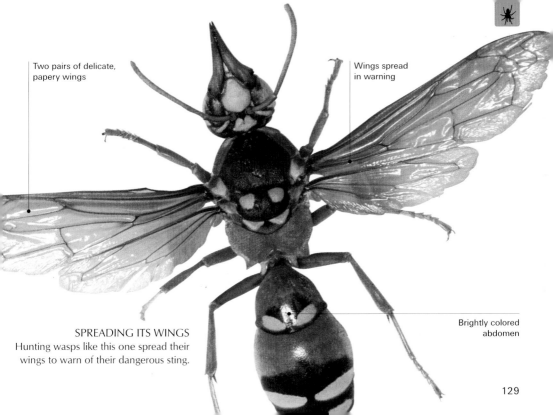

Two pairs of delicate, papery wings

Wings spread in warning

Brightly colored abdomen

SPREADING ITS WINGS
Hunting wasps like this one spread their wings to warn of their dangerous sting.

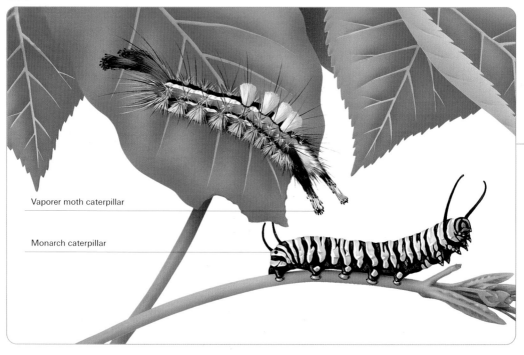

Vaporer moth caterpillar

Monarch caterpillar

Colorful Clues

The bright colors of many bugs are not just pretty to look at. In many cases, bugs display bright colors to warn potential attackers that they are unpleasant or even dangerous to eat. Warning colors are red, yellow, and orange—the same colors that humans use when we want to warn that something is dangerous. Bright colors and patterns are easily remembered, and predators quickly learn which bugs cannot be eaten.

POISONOUS INFANTS

Hairs on the vaporer moth caterpillar's body irritate the skin. The monarch caterpillar's insides are filled with chemicals that can kill its predators.

BLISTER BEETLE

These beetles ooze an irritating chemical that causes blisters.

STINKBUG

These bugs truly stink. They give out, or can spit, a foul-smelling liquid.

FIVE-SPOT BURNET MOTH

The bright red spots on this moth advertise its unpleasant taste.

Scare Tactics

Some bugs use scare tactics when under attack. One trick is to suddenly reveal large eyespots on an otherwise dull body. These spots can look like the larger eyes of an owl—a bird many small predators fear.

ORANGE FLASH
Only the males of the orange walking stick have these fan-shaped wings, which he flashes when threatened.

NIGHT EYES
The polyphemus moth flies only at night. Its dull brown wings blend perfectly with the undergrowth, until the moth is startled into revealing its huge blue and yellow eyespots.

Chemical Warfare

If warning signals and scare tactics do not frighten predators, chemical warfare often can. Insects like stinkbugs have special glands that repel attackers. Some stick insects spray foul liquid directly at enemies' faces.

PUSS MOTH DEFENSE
This caterpillar first inflates its head and raises two horns. It then can squirt acid from a gland beneath its head.

LETTING OFF STEAM

The bombardier beetle releases chemicals into a chamber in its abdomen. These react to make a hot substance that squirts out of the beetle with loud explosions.

BLOODY-NOSED BEETLE

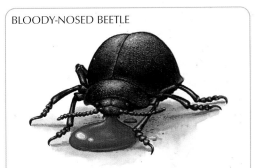

When disturbed, this beetle breaks thin membranes in its mouth to force out a droplet of fluid. The fluid contains chemicals that can make an attacker sick.

Camouflage

The best way to avoid being eaten is to avoid being noticed. A well-camouflaged bug blends into its surroundings. It may look just like the rocks, leaves, bark, or flowers on which it is resting.

HIDDEN IN THE LEAVES

When it stays perfectly still, the wings of the Southeast Asian geometer moth look very much like leaves.

ONE-STEP DEFENSE
When resting, dull-colored peanut bugs look almost identical to tree trunks.

TWO-STEP DEFENSE
But if the bug is spotted by a hungry bird, it snaps open its wings to flash two eyespots.

Look Closely

In this typical garden scene, there are 13 species of commonly found insects that use camouflage to hide themselves. Can you see how each insect is hidden?

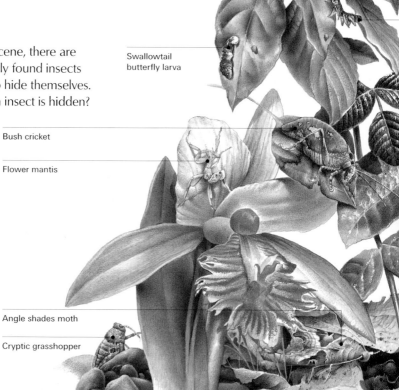

Swallowtail butterfly larva

Bush cricket

Flower mantis

Angle shades moth

Cryptic grasshopper

138

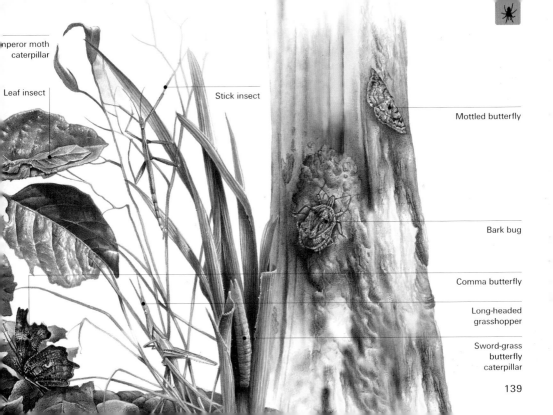

Emperor moth caterpillar

Leaf insect

Stick insect

Mottled butterfly

Bark bug

Comma butterfly

Long-headed grasshopper

Sword-grass butterfly caterpillar

Disguise

Bugs that are disguised use more than simple camouflage to hide from their enemies. Animals in disguise can be seen, but pretend to be something else. They usually mimic specific features in their habitat, such as sticks, leaves, flowers, and stones. Some stick insects, disguised as leaves, even sway gently in the breeze to complete the disguise.

DUNG DISGUISE
This female bird-dung spider pretends to be bird droppings during the day.

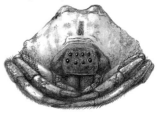

LIVING THORNS
The spiny shape of these thorn bugs, or treehoppers, makes it hard for birds to eat them. It is also an extremely effective disguise.

HANGING AROUND
This scorpion spider hangs in its web looking like a stray dead leaf.

A NEW LEAF
A long-legged leaf katydid's abdomen looks like the leaves among which it lives.

Hidden Hunters

Predators, too, can use camouflage and disguise when they are hunting. They either blend into their surroundings or disguise themselves as part of the habitat, and lie in ambush to spring upon unsuspecting prey.

AMBUSHING ASSASSIN
This orchid mantis slowly changes color from white to pink, and blends in almost perfectly with the flower. It sits very still, eyeing a katydid that has been attracted to the flower. When the katydid wanders within range, the mantis will lash out, its front legs snapping shut to clamp down on the katydid with sharp spines.

HOODED HUNTER
Leaf-shaped flaps cover the thorax and abdomen of the hooded leaf mantis. When combined with its mottled green color, these flaps provide an excellent disguise.

CAMOUFLAGED CRAB
Crab spiders keep quite still as they lurk among flowers with their front legs wide open. If a meal, such as this honeybee, lands within range, they strike instantly.

143

Clever Mimics

When creatures pretend to be part of their habitat, it is known as disguise. Mimicry involves one animal pretending to be another species of animal. Some bugs pretend to be dangerous by looking like a species that really is dangerous. Hover flies are harmless but they mimic stinging yellow jackets. Other bugs use mimicry to trick their prey into being eaten.

TRUE COLORS

Poisonous monarch butterfly

Harmless viceroy butterfly

Viceroy mimics the monarch so predators stay away

Black transverse band on each hindwing

Monarch warns it is dangerous with bold orange colors.

Lacks black transverse band.

DID YOU KNOW?
Some beetle larvae mimic bees, and trick male bees into taking them back to the hive.

DEADLY MATE

Some female fireflies mimic the flashing patterns of other species of fireflies to lure males as prey.

SPIDER OR WASP?

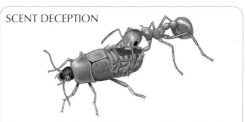

This jumping spider from Borneo mimics the Asian mutillid wasp, which has a painful sting.

ANT ANTICS

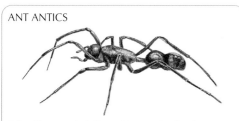

A Brazilian ant-mimicking spider uses its disguise to get close to the ants it looks like, then eats them.

SCENT DECEPTION

The ant-nest beetle mimics by scent to fool wood ants into giving it food, believing the beetle is from their colony.

Repelling Invaders

There are a number of ways bugs defend their homes from invaders. Some kinds of spiders hide in burrows topped with trap doors, which they hold closed if attacked. Ant and termite colonies have soldiers whose job is to protect the colony from invaders, no matter how large or small.

BOTTOM FIRST
This North American trap-door spider has been discovered by a wasp. It plugs its burrow with its leathery abdomen. This is hard to grip and protects the spider from stings.

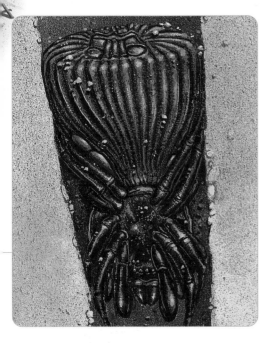

SOLDIERS ON GUARD
Nasute termite soldiers guard their colony. Their heads are sharpened to a point that can be used as a weapon. They can also squirt a sticky substance to discourage invaders.

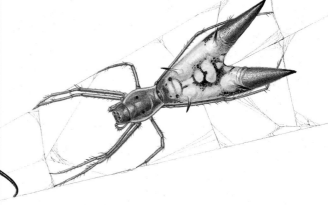

SHARP AND POINTY

The sharp points on the arrow-shaped spiny orb weaver's abdomen make it uncomfortable to swallow.

CURVED AND SPINY

The curved spined spider has unusual hornlike spines on its abdomen.

Odd Spiders

These spiders have developed spines, horns, spikes, and knobs to keep themselves out of danger.

LONG AND THIN
A narrow body means that the long-jawed orb weaver can hide by lying flat along a grass stem.

HARD AND SPIKY
This Micrathena spider's body is hard like a shell and difficult to eat.

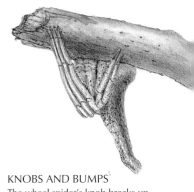

KNOBS AND BUMPS
The wheel spider's knob breaks up its body to make it harder to see.

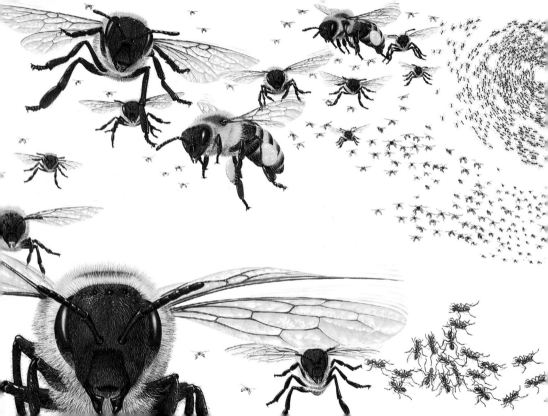

Strength in Numbers

The sheer number of creatures in a swarm of insects is sometimes the best defense of all. Even if some individuals die or are eaten, the vast majority will live to reproduce, and the species will survive. Some go even further. Social insects, such as these bees and ants, send complex messages to each other using chemicals. This allows them to coordinate their attacks on predators.

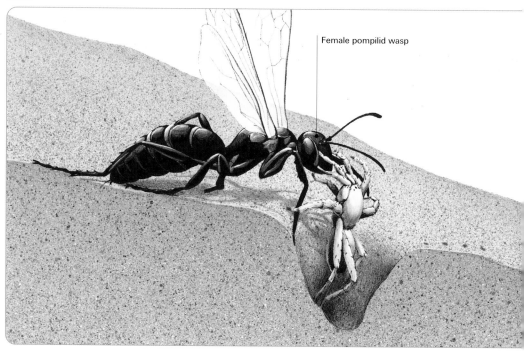

Female pompilid wasp

Some bugs have unusual ways of protecting themselves. It is hard to grab onto an insect or spider that is curled into a ball. Their backs can be armored to add to their defense.

ROLLING AWAY

Namib wheel spiders are the only animals that can build burrows in the sand. When this female wasp digs up a spider to lay her eggs on it, the spider has a trick to play. It breaks free, curls its legs, and spins away like a wheel.

KATYDID CONFUSION

When disturbed, this mountain katydid spreads its wings to look larger, and curls its abdomen to reveal startling, bright colors.

FOLLOW YOUR NOSE
The giant anteater sniffs out columns of ants with its keen sense of smell. When it finds them, the anteater uses its long tongue to slurp them into its mouth.

Preying on Bugs

Almost all bugs are prey to other animals. Larger land animals lick, suck, and gulp insects and spiders as part of, or all of, their diet. Fish, too, can eat bugs—the archer fish shoots water like an arrow to catch and devour insects.

A GREAT LEAP
Frogs use their powerful back legs and flick their tongues to catch prey.

GRAY WAGTAIL

Insects form most of the gray wagtail's diet, but the wagtail also eats small fish like minnows.

155

Stuck on You

This chameleon has been creeping slowly toward its insect prey. When it is close enough, it shoots out its incredibly long tongue, which is covered in sticky mucus. It then pulls back the tongue just as quickly, sling-shotting the insect into its mouth.

Bug Mouths

Inside a bug's mouth are the tools it uses for feeding. These are shaped to collect and eat their particular food. Flies pour their saliva over a spongy pad to dissolve the food so they can suck it up. Female mosquitoes have needle-like mouthparts to suck blood. Different spiders have jaws that move either up and down or side to side.

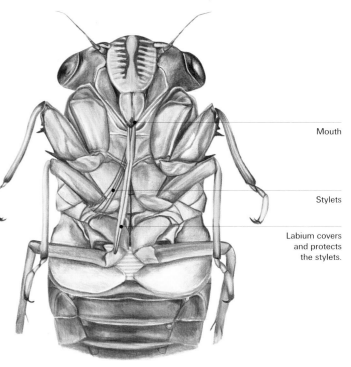

Mouth

Stylets

Labium covers and protects the stylets.

A BUG'S MOUTHPARTS
The stylets are used to pierce the food. The stylets then add saliva to partly digest the food before sucking it up.

158

A GRASSHOPPER'S MOUTHPARTS

Plant eaters chew or suck their food. Grasshoppers eat plants, chewing them with their strong jaws. These have sharp edges, ideal for cutting the tough grasses they eat.

A BEETLE'S MOUTHPARTS

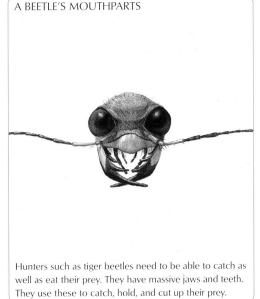

Hunters such as tiger beetles need to be able to catch as well as eat their prey. They have massive jaws and teeth. They use these to catch, hold, and cut up their prey.

Insect Predators

A praying mantis will sit and wait patiently for its next victim to land nearby. Then, with lightning speed, it strikes out with its superfast front legs. The legs snap shut, gripping the prey on their sharp spines. Even though the victim is struggling to free itself, the mantis will sometimes start feeding on it while it is still alive.

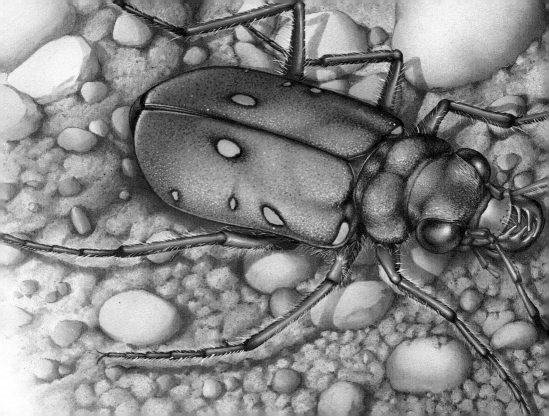

Tiger Beetle on the Hunt

Tiger beetles chase and catch ants to eat. They use their enormous jaws to snatch and crush the ants. Then the beetles devour them. These speedy insects can move 18 inches (50 cm) per second. Only cockroaches run faster.

Spider Predators

Instead of webs, some spiders use stealth or tricks to catch their prey. Crab spiders rely on disguise to catch prey. Trap-door spiders use secret doors. They fling open the door and grab the surprised victim as it passes by.

FISHING SPIDER
These spiders live near water, and catch tiny fish and insects.

HUNTSMAN SPIDER
This spider hunts at night and pounces on its insect prey.

TARANTULA STRIKES
This large spider catches mice.
It also eats frogs, small birds,
lizards, and young snakes.

Traps and Lures

Insects and spiders use some ingenious methods to lure prey. Poison, traps, and tricks may help some of them catch their next meal. Others lure their victims to their death by flashing pretty lights or using attractive scents.

SPIT AND GRAB TACTICS

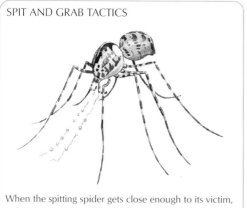

When the spitting spider gets close enough to its victim, it shoots out sticky venom to trap and paralyze it.

GLOW-IN-THE-DARK TRAP

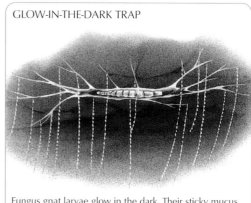

Fungus gnat larvae glow in the dark. Their sticky mucus threads catch any insects that are attracted to the light.

THE ANT TRAP
Antlion larvae, also called doodlebugs, live buried at the base of a pit trap into which ants and other small prey fall.

ANTLION
Only the larvae of antlions feed, so they need to eat enough food to keep them alive as adults.

Hunting Underwater

Many bugs live in or near rivers, ponds, creeks, and even puddles. They hunt in ways that are specific to their watery homes. Some spiders hunt prey on the surface of ponds. Diving beetles are among the few insects strong enough to kill small vertebrates like fish, tadpoles, or frogs. Dragonfly nymphs hunt underwater, but the adults roam the air.

FROG CATCHER
Giant water bugs can catch small frogs.

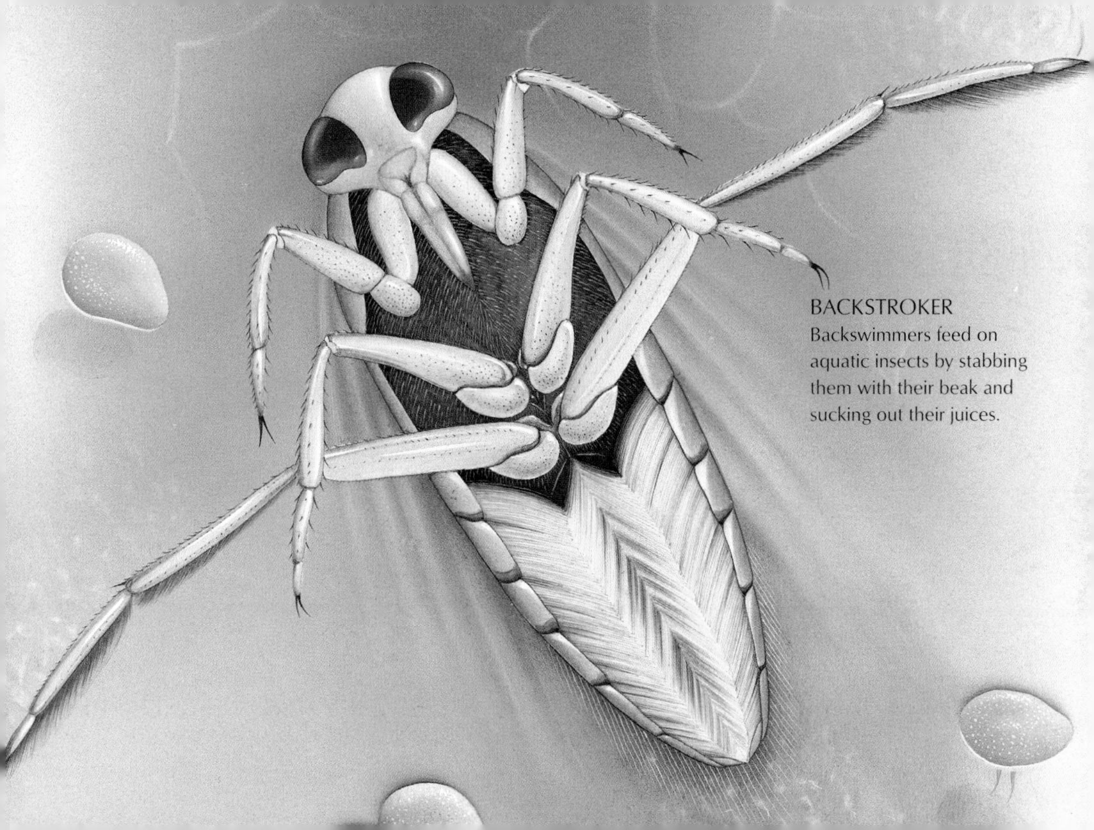

BACKSTROKER
Backswimmers feed on aquatic insects by stabbing them with their beak and sucking out their juices.

Webs for Hunting

Spiders make silk for lining burrows, to wrap eggs or prey, and to make draglines for traveling. But the most amazing use of silk is to build webs to trap unwary insects that fly into them. When its web is complete, the spider simply waits until its next meal is trapped.

WRAPS FOR DINNER
Some spiders wrap their freshly caught meal in spider silk. They store it to eat later on.

DID YOU KNOW?
Spider silk is much stronger than steel. It could be used to make bullet-proof vests.

CASTING NETS
A net-casting spider builds nets out of silk. It hurls this net onto an insect to trap it, then scoops it in.

Flower Feeders

The tongues of butterflies and moths are made especially for drinking the nectar of flowers. They are very long—they curl up when not being used and uncurl to drink. They are rather like drinking straws.

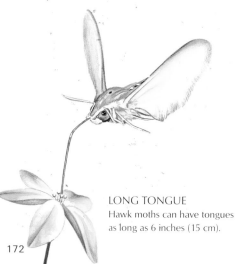

LONG TONGUE
Hawk moths can have tongues as long as 6 inches (15 cm).

SWEATING IT OUT
Sweat bees have short, pointed tongues and feed on shallow flowers. They live in underground cells.

A COLORFUL LURE
Flowers have bright colors, including some we cannot see, to lure insects. Some flowers even have landing platforms.

A FEAST OF NECTAR
Acacias provide butterflies, such as this marine blue, with plentiful nectar.

Making Honey

Bees make honey to feed their hive. One hive of honeybees can make about 110 pounds (50 kg) of honey a year. To make honey, they force nectar out of their honey stomach and mix it with spit.

POLLEN DUSTER
Bees visit flowers to gather nectar and pollen, so they can make honey.

PICKING UP POLLEN
Bumblebees fly off to visit many flowers before they return to their colony, brushing pollen onto each plant they visit.

SWAPPING SPIT
Honeymaking starts when bumblebees return to the nest. The bees spit up nectar together to make honey.

Cleaning Up

Imagine eating dung! Some beetle larvae do. After the dung is rolled into balls, the female lays one or more eggs in it. When the larvae hatch, they eat the dung. This helps clean up the waste products of other animals.

ROLY POLY
Both male and female dung beetles carry out the important job of rolling the dung into balls to prepare it for their eggs.

KITCHEN SCAVENGERS
Cockroaches will eat any food scraps they find, but they can go without food for months.

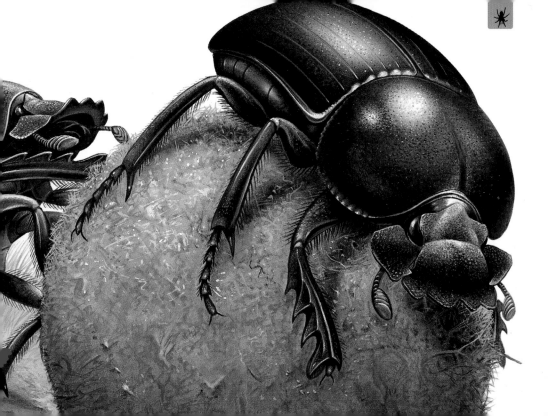

Filling the Larder

Leaf-cutter ants are farmers. Medium-sized workers carry leaf pieces to the nest while small worker ants fend off flies. Soldier ants guard the leaves, which workers take below to make compost to grow the fungus they eat.

Small worker ant

Soldier ant

Worker ant

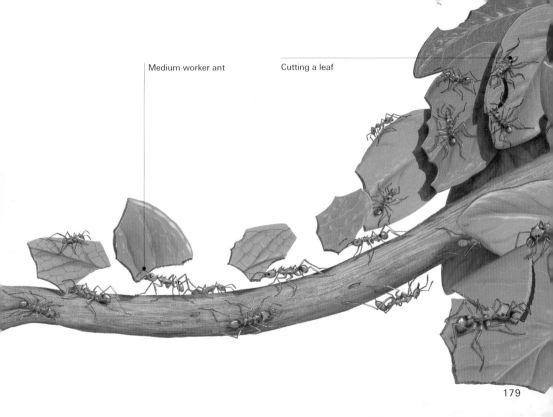

Medium worker ant

Cutting a leaf

Living off Others

Many bugs are blood suckers—they find a host and feast on its blood. Some can detect the body heat of a passing host. They pierce the skin and bloodstream using needle-like mouthparts, and then suck. Mosquitoes and ticks keep sucking until their bellies are almost bursting.

TICKED OFF
Ticks attach themselves to animals or people as they brush past them.

HUMAN FLEA

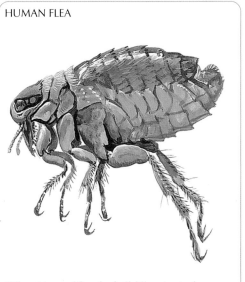

Different types of fleas feed off different animals, so there are cat fleas, dog fleas, and this one, a human flea.

PUBIC LOUSE

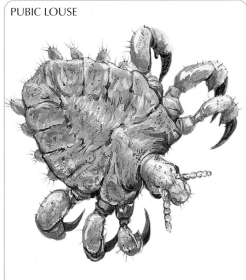

These tiny insects attach their eggs to the pubic hair of humans and gorillas. A biting adult causes itching.

How Flies Eat

Flies eat all kinds of food, some by sucking blood, others by infesting rotting fruit, decaying flesh, or dung. Some flies have mouths like a sponge so they can eat only liquid. They vomit saliva all over food to dissolve it, then they suck up the mush. Fly larvae, called maggots, eat dead plants and animals.

NECTAR SLURPER

The hairy bee uses long, needle-like mouthparts to drink nectar.

BLOOD SUCKER

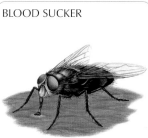

Tsetse flies suck the blood of cows and people until their bellies swell.

FRUIT INFESTER

Fruit flies eat rotting fruit. Swarms can be seen around fallen fruit.

ATTACK IN MIDAIR

The ultrafast robber fly can snatch a bee in midair. Then it stabs the bee with its mouthparts to kill it.

183

Bugs and Plants

Some bugs have special relationships with plants. Many plants need bugs to pollinate, or fertilize, them. The yucca moth caterpillar needs yucca seeds to feed itself, and the yucca plant needs the moth to pollinate it. Ants living on the bullhorn acacia chase away anything that might harm the plant. In return, acacia pods provide the ants with a home.

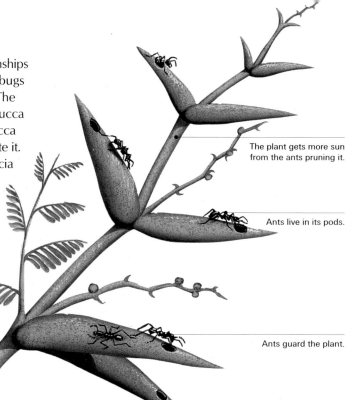

The plant gets more sun from the ants pruning it.

Ants live in its pods.

Bullhorn acacia

Ants guard the plant.

184

MEXICAN JUMPING BEANS

When the Mexican moth caterpillar gets hot, it jerks about to drag the bean it lives inside into the shade.

PARTNERS IN LIFE
Yucca moths and yucca plants depend on each other to survive.

Bees and Plants

Plants need bees to pollinate them and bees need flowers for nectar to make honey. Bees get covered in pollen when they visit a flower, which brushes off on other flowers, and pollinates those that are the same species.

SETTING POLLEN TRAPS

Plants need pollen to reproduce. Pollen attaches easily to the hairs on a bee's body and legs.

LURING THE BEE

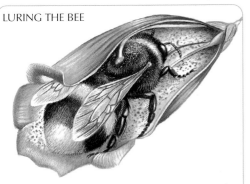

Long, thin flowers like foxgloves force the bee to crawl inside for nectar, ensuring it gets well dusted with pollen.

MOVING POLLEN AROUND

As a bee goes from flower to flower, it leaves pollen behind.

Feeding on Plants

Plants supply food for many different kinds of insects and spiders. They provide leaves, bark, wood, flowers, stems, sap, and even the fungus that grows on them. Some large plants, such as rain forest trees, have thriving communities of hundreds of different bugs, each with its own special kind of food, all provided by a single tree.

LEAFY FEAST
These beetle larvae work closely side by side, eating away a leaf. They rarely eat the leaf's veins.

DRILLING FOR FOOD

Acorn weevils bore into nuts.

FUNGUS FEEDER

Horned fungus beetles eat fungus.

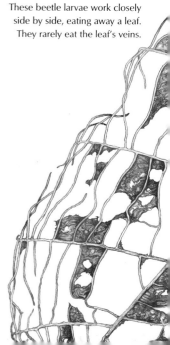

Turning the Tables

Insects eat plants, but some plants eat insects, too. They may lure them with pretty colors and patterns, or even offer landing platforms. Then they trap the insects and feed on them.

A PITCH INTO DEATH
Pitcher plants have tubes filled with liquid that insects fall into and die.

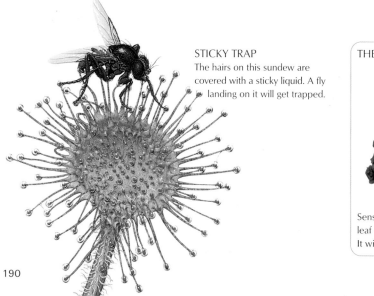

STICKY TRAP
The hairs on this sundew are covered with a sticky liquid. A fly landing on it will get trapped.

THE JAWS OF DEATH

Sensitive hairs on a venus flytrap leaf detect an insect landing on it. It will snap shut, trapping the bug.

INSIDE THE TRAP
Some canny animals live inside pitcher
plants to steal the insects they catch.

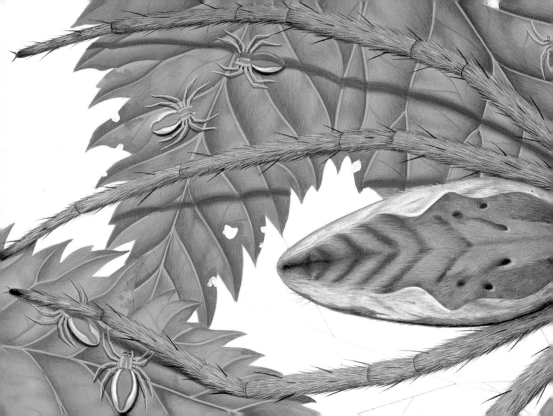

A BUG'S LIFE

Reproducing Bugs

Bugs need to reproduce, just like all other animals. However, young insects go through various life stages before they become adults. This process is called metamorphosis, and it can occur in three or four stages, depending on the insect. Spiders reproduce by laying eggs that hatch as miniature versions of the adult.

ADULTS ONLY
Like all bugs, beetles are ready to mate only when they become adults.

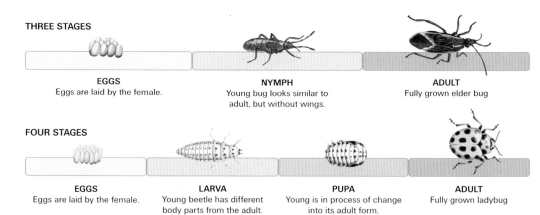

THREE STAGES

EGGS
Eggs are laid by the female.

NYMPH
Young bug looks similar to adult, but without wings.

ADULT
Fully grown elder bug

FOUR STAGES

EGGS
Eggs are laid by the female.

LARVA
Young beetle has different body parts from the adult.

PUPA
Young is in process of change into its adult form.

ADULT
Fully grown ladybug

Fighting for a Mate

Locking their horns, two male Hercules beetles fight over the right to mate with a female. The fight seems quite ferocious but they rarely hurt each other badly. The loser usually just runs away.

Insect Courtship

DANCING PARTNERS

During the courtship of the dance fly, the male offers a mosquito he has caught to the female. She eats this meal while mating takes place.

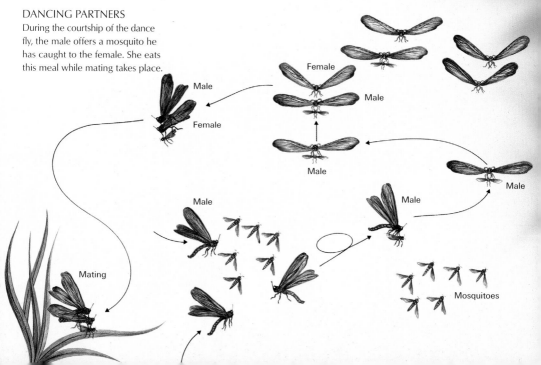

Male

Female

Female

Male

Male

Male

Male

Male

Male

Mating

Mosquitoes

COURTING ON THE WING

A male hoverfly follows a female, from above and behind, and shadows her until she lands. He then lands on top of her to mate.

Spider Courtship

Spiders court in many ways. Some spiders send messages by tapping the web using special signals. Wolf and jumping spiders perform elaborate dances. The female green spider will attach a silk line to a leaf and leap into the air. The male follows on his line and they mate while hanging in midair. Many female spiders eat the male after mating.

DID YOU KNOW?

Some male crab spiders tie up the female with silk so they can mate with her.

JUMPING SPIDER COURTING

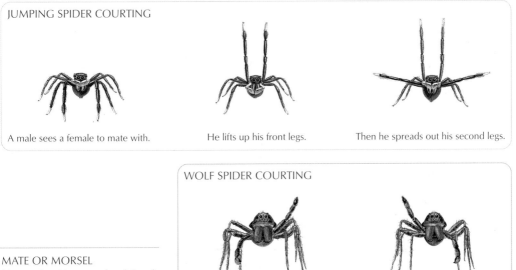

A male sees a female to mate with.

He lifts up his front legs.

Then he spreads out his second legs.

WOLF SPIDER COURTING

The male waves a leg.

Then he waves another leg.

MATE OR MORSEL

Many male spiders tap a female's web in a special pattern to show they are not the female's next meal.

Scorpion Courtship

Scorpions are related to spiders and, like them, they have eight legs. In addition, they have large pedipalps that end in grasping pincers. The male and female sometimes join pincers and perform a courtship dance before mating takes place. Like other arachnids, males are sometimes eaten after mating.

CLASPING PINCERS
These scorpions "dance" to find a level piece of ground, so the male can deposit his sperm somewhere flat for the female to pick up.

Mating

Bugs get together to mate before the female can lay her eggs. A male insect mostly delivers his sperm to the female in a packet that he puts into the female's genital opening. Male spiders transfer sperm using a syringe-like structure on their pedipalps. Mating can be particularly tricky for the many insects that perform the act while flying.

GETTING TOGETHER
Mating can last anywhere from a few seconds to many hours, depending on the kind of insect.

Laying Eggs

Nearly all bugs lay eggs, but some give birth to live young. The eggs are usually laid near a source of food, often a plant suitable for the young to eat. Females can lay a single egg but it is more common that clusters of hundreds, or even thousands, are laid.

UNLUCKY HOST

This female ichneumon wasp finds a larva of a wood wasp. She drills a hole into the branch and stings the larva, then deposits her egg directly onto it. Her egg will hatch and then feed on its wood wasp host.

MOSQUITO

Eggs are laid in clusters on a pond. These float like a raft.

COCKROACH

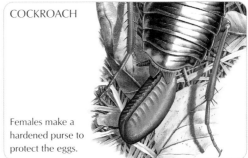

Females make a hardened purse to protect the eggs.

ANT

The queen lays the eggs; the workers care for them.

LADYBUG

Females lay bright yellow eggs on a leaf.

Eggs and Egg Sacs

Egg sacs are made out of silk. Female spiders lay a few to a few hundred eggs in their sacs. The sac protects the eggs from getting too wet or too dry. It also makes it more difficult for predators to get at the eggs and eat them. A sac can be placed in a web, under bark, or on a leaf. The female sometimes carries it around.

WOLF SPIDER EXPRESS
Even after the eggs hatch, the spiderlings continue to ride on the female wolf spider's back until their first molt.

BLACK WIDOW'S PURSE
A female black widow can lay up to 20 eggs. She secures them in a silk sac, and attaches this to her web.

PORTABLE EGGS
To protect her eggs, this female wolf spider carries her egg sac on her body, attached to her spinnerets.

On Their Own

When spiderlings leave their sac or web, many use threads of silk as sails. They send out a silk line to catch the wind and then launch themselves from the tops of plants. This is known as ballooning. They also use silk to make draglines to move themselves around plants.

210

Nymph to Adult

Insects that change three times go from egg, to nymph, to adult. Nymphs mostly look like smaller versions of adults, but with buds instead of wings. Nymphs undergo several molts until they become fully grown adults.

DID YOU KNOW?

Periodical cicada nymphs live underground for up to 17 years before emerging.

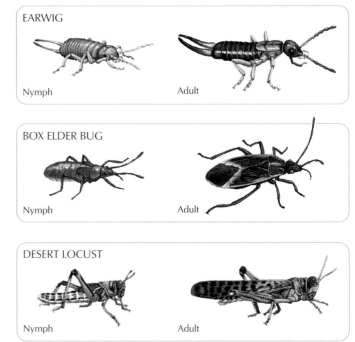

EARWIG

Nymph   Adult

BOX ELDER BUG

Nymph   Adult

DESERT LOCUST

Nymph   Adult

CICADA EMERGING
An adult cicada emerges from its final nymph's exoskeleton.

Dragonfly Life Cycle

Although adults live in the air and are skilled flyers, the nymphs of dragonflies have a totally different life. They live underwater for up to five years before leaving the water. When they leave, they have one final molt before flying off.

LIFE CYCLE OF A DRAGONFLY

1 Mating (male at top)
2 Egg laying (female)
3 Nymphs emerging from eggs
4 Nymph hunting underwater
5 Nymph leaving the water
6 Final molt
7 Adult dragonfly

2

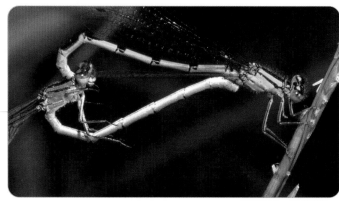

MATING THE DRAGONFLY WAY
The bright blue male grips the female behind her head before mating occurs.

214

1. FEMALE LAYS EGGS; THESE HATCH

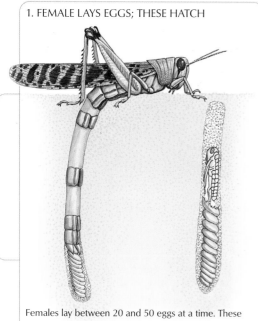

Females lay between 20 and 50 eggs at a time. These hatch into nymphs, which burrow to the surface to feed.

2. NYMPH FEEDS

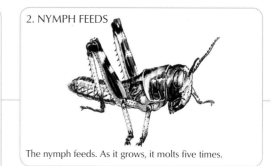

The nymph feeds. As it grows, it molts five times.

6. ADULTS BREED

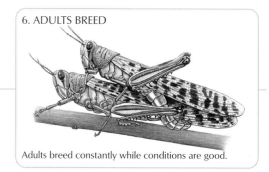

Adults breed constantly while conditions are good.

Desert Locust Life Cycle

Desert locusts are usually solitary insects but when conditions are right, the adults keep breeding, the nymphs keep hatching, and massive swarms of locusts form. These swarms can contain billions of insects.

3. NYMPH HAS FINAL MOLT

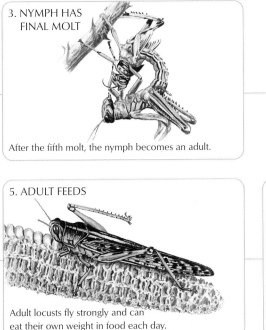

After the fifth molt, the nymph becomes an adult.

5. ADULT FEEDS

Adult locusts fly strongly and can eat their own weight in food each day.

4. NEW ADULTS EMERGE

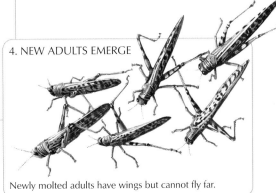

Newly molted adults have wings but cannot fly far.

Metamorphosis

Many insects undergo a transformation called metamorphosis. They start life as eggs that hatch into larvae, a stage where eating is the most important activity. The next stage is spent as pupae, where the insects transform into the final stage—adults.

PUPAL PROCESSES
This bee pupa is enclosed in a wax cell. The pupa completely destroys its larval body parts and rebuilds them as adult body parts.

LIFE STAGES
Ladybugs grow quickly and spend most of their lives as adults. But stag beetles spend most of their lives as larvae.

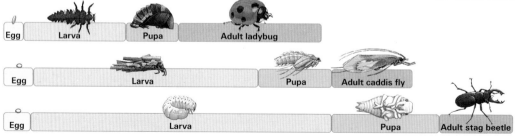

218

READY FOR LIFTOFF
After an adult butterfly emerges from its pupal case, it unfurls its new wings and flies off as soon as they are dry.

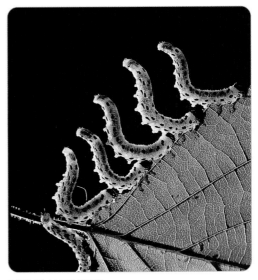

EATING MACHINES
The larvae of sawflies are greedy feeders. They spend their days chewing through leaves.

219

Atlas Moth Metamorphosis

An atlas moth lays eggs, which hatch into larvae. Feeding hungrily, the larvae grow larger over several molts, then make a cocoon in which they pupate. Once the transformation is complete, the adults break free, dry their wings, and fly away.

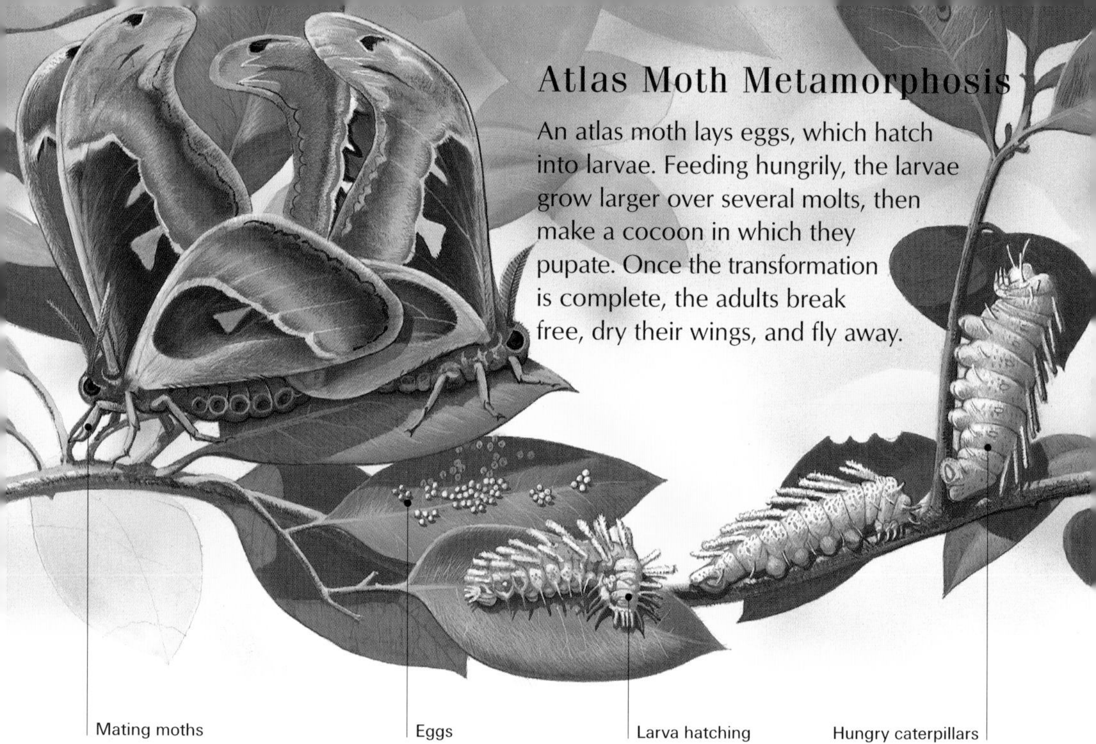

Mating moths

Eggs

Larva hatching

Hungry caterpillars

Pupating

Emerging adult

Adult flying off

Migrating Monarchs

Each fall, monarch butterflies fly 1,800 miles (2,900 km) from North America to Mexico. Here they winter and breed, before returning north in spring. They lay their eggs on the way, but die before completing their trip. The next generation completes the migration.

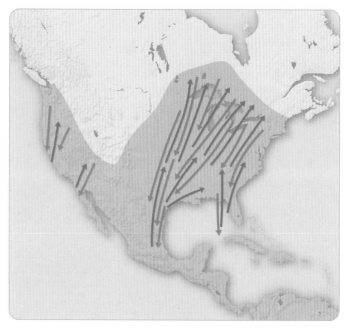

KEY
→ Fall migration
→ Spring migration
▨ Distribution

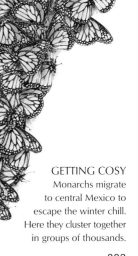

TREE-TO-TREE BUTTERFLIES
Clusters of monarch butterflies cover entire trees in Mexico.
The weight of the cluster helps protect them from the wind.

GETTING COSY
Monarchs migrate
to central Mexico to
escape the winter chill.
Here they cluster together
in groups of thousands.

BUGS
AND US

Insects in Ancient China

Silk has been made in China for thousands of years. Chinese people used silk to write and paint on, to make into clothes and bags, and to trade.

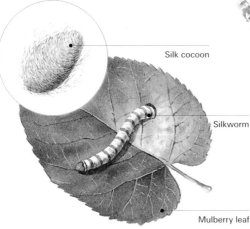

Silk cocoon

Silkworm

Mulberry leaf

FARMING SILK

Mulberry leaves were gathered by hand and fed to the caterpillars.

UNRAVELING COCOONS

Cocoons were rinsed in hot water to loosen the threads of silk before the emerging moths could bite their way out.

PRECIOUS GIFTS

Chinese emperors presented delicately embroidered, beautifully woven pieces of silk to neighboring countries.

DUNG FOR DINNER

This scarab beetle is rolling a ball of dung. The female lays her eggs inside, then the newly hatched larvae will eat it up.

THE BEETLE-FACED GOD

The god Kephri had a scarab face. Egyptians believed he rolled out the Sun each day, the way a scarab beetle rolls dung.

Insects in Ancient Egypt

Ancient Egyptians revered an animal that eats dung. They worshipped a Sun god, and, to them, the beetle's action of rolling dung across the earth was like the Sun moving across the sky.

TREASURES
Some ancient Egyptian jewelry, like this chest piece, contains scarab beetles made from precious stones.

Venoms and Stings

DIVING IN FOR THE STING
Wasps are superbly adapted as flying predators. Their stings can be very painful, and they can sting their victim over and over again.

TAIL STINGER
A scorpion has a stinger on its tail.
All are venomous, but few are deadly.

While most insects and spiders are harmless to people, some do bite or sting. These include wasps, ants, flies, mosquitoes, lice, bed bugs, mites, ticks, spiders, and scorpions. Most sting to subdue prey or to defend themselves.

DANGEROUS FANGS
The female redback spider has stronger venom than the smaller male redback.

Stingers

Ants, wasps, and bees are among the most advanced insects, and many of them have stingers. They are used to inject venom into their prey to stun or kill them, and also to defend themselves or their nest. Some bees die after just one sting, because their stinger has a barb that pulls out their insides when they try to fly off.

OUCH!
A wasp sting can cause a burning pain and swelling.

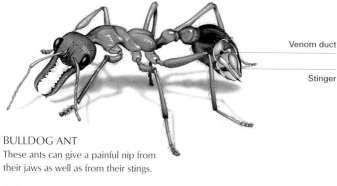

Venom duct

Stinger

BULLDOG ANT
These ants can give a painful nip from their jaws as well as from their stings.

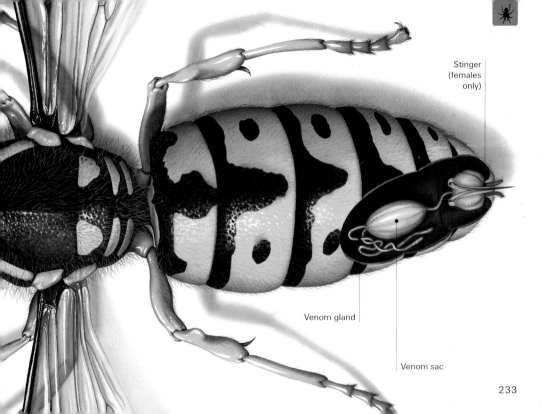

Stinger
(females
only)

Venom gland

Venom sac

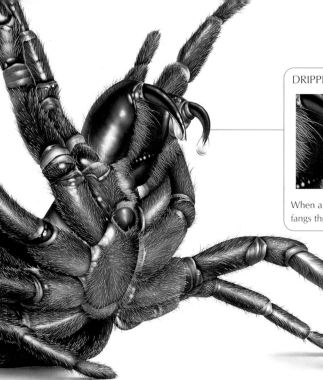

DRIPPING FANGS

When a spider bites, venom flows from glands in the fangs through ducts that end in small holes at the tips.

Fangs and Jaws

One way to deliver a shot of venom is by stabbing the victim with sharp fangs and pumping the poison directly into its flesh. Spiders that do this, like tarantulas and their relatives, have large, piercing, downward-stabbing fangs. Other spiders have fangs that face sideways.

THE GENTLE RED-KNEED TARANTULA
Some spiders that look dangerous are actually quite docile. A tarantula has a bite that is no more painful than a bee sting. It is not poisonous to humans.

DID YOU KNOW?

Some spider bites cause the area around the bitten flesh to die and then decay.

Good Bugs, Bad Bugs

People love to hate bugs. Some eat our food plants, but others are necessary to pollinate them. Spiders may seem scary, but they eat pest insects and are themselves food for birds.

RUINING LUNCH
Fruit can be spoilt by feeding insects, such as this wasp.

KEEPING PLANTS ALIVE
Pollinating insects are essential for plants to reproduce.

WALKING PESTICIDE
Spiders eat insects, so they can help control pests.

Crop and Food Pests

Some insects eat our crops and other plants we grow for food. Others invade our homes, such as the cockroaches, flies, and ants that devour food left lying around. Some insects, ticks, and mites attack farm animals, causing loss of condition and disease.

POTATO THIEF
The Colorado beetle eats potatoes and destroys crops worldwide.

GARDENER'S PEST
Tiny aphids feed by sucking juices out of stems and leaves. They also spread disease among plants.

Plagues of Insects

Insects that breed in massive numbers then swarm together form a plague. Locusts normally act alone, but during a plague they start to behave as a group, eating their way through vast amounts of plants.

GIANT EATING MACHINE
A swarm of 500,000 locusts can eat up to a ton of food daily.

LOCUST SWARM
In certain conditions, individual locusts form massive feeding groups.

DID YOU KNOW?

A single square mile (3 sq km) of swarming locusts can contain billions of insects.

SNAP-SHUT JAWS
Tropical trapjaw ants have massive jaws that snap painfully shut when something touches them.

WHINING IN YOUR EAR
Mosquitoes buzz about in the dark, circling to find you by sensing body heat, humidity, odor, and breath.

RIDDLED WITH TICKS
Some types of ticks feed in clusters. As they feed, they inject their host with poison that can paralyze or even kill.

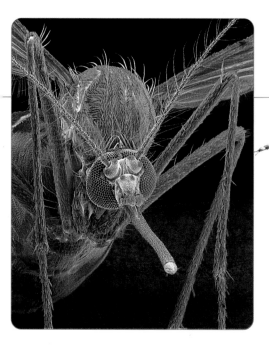

Biting Pests

Mites, bed bugs, and mosquitoes are blood feeders that bite using piercing mouthparts. They do this to suck blood for food. Other insects may bite to defend themselves.

Disease Carriers

Some insects carry diseases that have killed vast numbers of people. Malaria, which kills about 2 million people each year, is spread by mosquitoes. Bubonic plague wiped out a fourth of the world's people between 1346 and 1350. Insects also carry sleeping sickness and yellow fever, and transmit typhus.

BLACK RAT—BLACK DEATH

Rats carry fleas that spread bubonic plague, known as the black death.

YOU ARE GETTING SLEEPY

Tsetse flies suck so much blood they get grossly swollen bellies. They also spread African sleeping sickness.

FEVERED TICK

Deer ticks spread Lyme disease, an illness that causes a distinctive bull's-eye rash and fever.

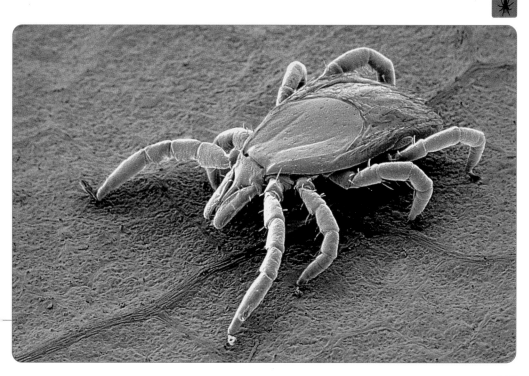

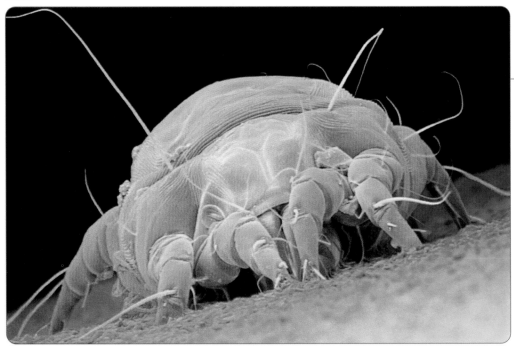

House Pests

Every house has a tiny bug zoo within. While many bugs just come and go, others can be a nuisance at best, or destructive at worst. They eat our stored food, clothes, carpets, books, and furniture. Termites even eat the house itself. Some bugs come inside to feed on us.

BREATHLESS BEAST
Dust mites are known to trigger asthma attacks.

KITCHEN BEAST

Hardy cockroaches can survive 42 days without food.

HOMEWORK-EATING BEAST
Silverfish can wriggle into tiny places, even in between the pages of a book, where they will eat the paper and glue.

Good Bugs

Without insects and spiders, we would not survive. That is because so many of the plants we eat depend on insects for pollination. A plant that is pollinated produces seeds to make more plants. In some cultures, ants and crickets are eaten. Silkworms are farmed to make silk fabrics.

HOW SWEET IT IS
Many insects love the sweet nectar of flowers and are important pollinators.

THE EXTERMINATORS
Ladybugs are welcomed by gardeners because they eat aphids, which are pests that destroy garden plants.

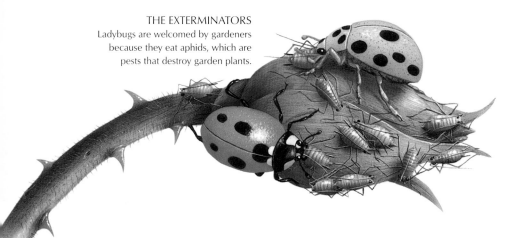

Humans and the Honeypot

Honeybees can be farmed for their honey. When beekeepers want to start a new hive, they catch a queen and put her in a special box for a hive. Many of the worker bees from the old hive will follow her to set up the new colony.

COLLECTING THE HONEY
Beekeepers wear special suits and spray hives with smoke to avoid stings.

THE OLD QUEEN LEAVES

When a new queen is raised, the old queen will leave the hive.

WORKERS STAND BY

Many worker bees will swarm with her, searching for a new home.

A HANDY NEW HOME

When a new home is found, the queen and the workers move in.

Studying Bugs

Catching bugs in the air or on the ground is easy. You can then observe or take pictures of them before they are released. Use a clear plastic container to catch them, so that you are not stung or bitten accidently. Bugs are very fragile, so if you have to pick them up, do so carefully to avoid damaging their bodies.

CATCHING TREE DWELLERS
Put a white sheet under a tree, then shake the branches to see what falls.

BEETLE MANIA
The huge variety of beetles
makes them popular to study.

HOW TO CATCH BUGS
Catch an insect or spider by placing a clear container over
it. Then slide a flat lid or board underneath and turn it over.

GRASSHOPPERS
Grasshoppers have large back wings that remain hidden when they are not flying.

Collecting Bugs

Insects and spiders are easy to observe in their natural environment, but when that is not practical, they can be collected and observed at home. See if you can identify what you have caught before you release it.

SWALLOWTAIL BUTTERFLIES

Swallowtails have long-tailed wings.

GOLIATH BEETLES

These can grow to several inches.

STICK INSECTS

These resemble branches of plants.

Keeping Bugs as Pets

Insects and spiders are low maintenance, cheap pets that are good for any type of home. Unusual pets like beetles, stick insects, and praying mantises are fun to keep. Many have bizarre shapes or pretty colors. An aquarium or terrarium with a fine mesh lid makes a suitable cage. Add a vase to hold food plants.

SCARY, HAIRY PETS
Tarantulas are long-lived and make excellent furry pets. They are not allowed to be sold in some countries, so they are not available to everyone.

FEEDING INSECTS
Keep your insect in a jar or aquarium with air holes. Make sure there is enough water, and that there is the right sort of food for your bug to eat.

DID YOU KNOW?

For over 2,000 years, singing and fighting crickets have been popular pets in China.

KINDS OF BUGS

Spiders

JUMPING SPIDERS

RED-HEADED MOUSE SPIDER

FAST FACTS

Class: Arachnida

Order: Araneae

Family: Salticidae

Scientific name:
Unknown*

Diet: Small arthropods

Location: Worldwide

Jumping spiders hunt during the day, leaping with silk draglines behind them. They have large forward-facing eyes for good vision.

The illustration is a general image of the group rather than an individual species.

FAST FACTS

Class: Arachnida

Order: Araneae

Family: Actinopodidae

Scientific name:
Missulena insignis

Diet: Small arthropods

Location: Australia

Only male red-headed mouse spiders have such a red head and blue body. Females are dark brown or black, with reddish jaws.

GOLDEN SILK SPIDER

FAST FACTS

Class: Arachnida

Order: Araneae

Family: Argiopidae

Scientific name:

Nephila sp.

Diet: Flying insects

Location: Worldwide

These spiders build large orb webs of golden silk, which can measure more than 3 feet (1 m) across and are suspended between trees.

SYDNEY FUNNEL-WEB SPIDER

FAST FACTS

Class: Arachnida

Order: Araneae

Family: Dipluridae

Scientific name:

Atrax robustus

Diet: Insects, lizards

Location: Australia

These aggressive spiders live under rocks or in burrows lined with silk. The venom of male funnel-webs can be deadly to humans.

Spiders

HUNTSMAN SPIDER

FAST FACTS

Class: Arachnida

Order: Araneae

Family: Sparassidae

Scientific name:
Unknown

Diet: Insects, arthropods

Location: Warm regions

The legs of huntsman spiders have joints that allow these prowling hunters to move quickly in all directions.

VIOLIN SPIDER

FAST FACTS

Class: Arachnida

Order: Araneae

Family: Loxoscelidae

Scientific name:
Loxosceles reclusa

Diet: Insects, arthropods

Location: North America

Violin spiders are named because of the distinctive violin pattern on their cephalothorax. They are also called brown recluses.

CRAB SPIDER

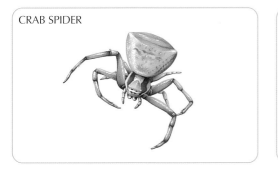

FAST FACTS

Class: Arachnida

Order: Araneae

Family: Thomisidae

Scientific name:
Unknown

Diet: Small insects

Location: Worldwide

These spiders look and even move like crabs. Some are brightly colored and wait inside flowers to snatch prey with their front legs.

BRAZILIAN WANDERING SPIDER

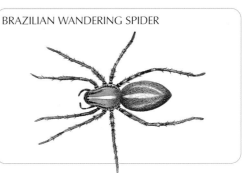

FAST FACTS

Class: Arachnida

Order: Araneae

Family: Ctenidae

Scientific name:
Phoneutria fera

Diet: Insects, small mice

Location: South America

This spider is poisonous to humans. It lives in plant matter and on the ground. It wanders about, rather than living in a web.

Spiders

TARANTULA

FAST FACTS

Class: Arachnida

Order: Araneae

Family: Theraphosidae

Scientific name:
Unknown

Diet: Insects, frogs, mice

Location: Amercias

Tarantulas were named because their bite was thought to cause tarantism, which made people weep and dance wildly.

LYNX SPIDER

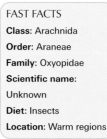

FAST FACTS

Class: Arachnida

Order: Araneae

Family: Oxyopidae

Scientific name:
Unknown

Diet: Insects

Location: Warm regions

Lynx spiders are so called because they pounce on their insect prey like lynxes do. They have six eyes and a tapered abdomen.

TRAP-DOOR SPIDER

FAST FACTS

Class: Arachnida
Order: Araneae
Family: Ctenizidae
Scientific name:
Unknown
Diet: Insects, arthropods
Location: Worldwide

These spiders build burrows in the ground, closed by a hinged door made from silk, plant matter, and soil. They snatch prey from just inside.

COMB-FOOTED SPIDER

FAST FACTS

Class: Arachnida
Order: Araneae
Family: Theridiidae
Scientific name:
Unknown
Diet: Insects
Location: Worldwide

Comb-footed spiders have comblike bristles on the feet of their back legs, which they use to wrap silk around their prey.

Spiders

SOUTHERN BLACK WIDOW

NORTHERN BLACK WIDOW

FAST FACTS

Class: Arachnida

Order: Araneae

Family: Theridiidae

Scientific name:

Latrodectus mactans

Diet: Insects

Location: North America

The southern black widow is one of the most feared spiders in the world. Yet this spider will bite a human only if provoked.

FAST FACTS

Class: Arachnida

Order: Araneae

Family: Theridiidae

Scientific name:

Latrodectus variolus

Diet: Insects

Location: North America

The northern black widow can be distinguished from its southern relative only by slightly different markings on its abdomen.

BROWN WIDOW

FAST FACTS

Class: Arachnida

Order: Araneae

Family: Theridiidae

Scientific name:
Latrodectus geometricus

Diet: Large insects

Location: Warm regions

These spiders will attack enemies only if their egg sac is threatened. The body is dark to light brown with reddish spots.

REDBACK SPIDER

FAST FACTS

Class: Arachnida

Order: Araneae

Family: Theridiidae

Scientific name:
Latrodectus hasselti

Diet: Insects

Location: Australia

Redback spiders build their webs in dry, sheltered areas, such as among rocks or logs, inside garden sheds, or even under outside toilet seats.

Other Arachnids

SCORPION

FAST FACTS

Class: Arachnida
Order: Scorpiones
Family: Unknown
Scientific name:
Unknown
Diet: Insects, arthropods
Location: Worldwide

Scorpions are the oldest group of arachnids. They live under rocks, logs, and bark during the day; they come out at dusk to feed.

HARD TICK

FAST FACTS

Class: Arachnida
Order: Acarina
Family: Ixodidae
Scientific name:
Unknown
Diet: Blood
Location: Worldwide

Ticks pierce the skin of their host with their barbed beak and suck blood. Some cause paralysis and death. Others transmit illnesses.

SUN SPIDER

FAST FACTS

Class: Arachnida

Order: Solifugae

Family: Unknown

Scientific name:
Unknown

Diet: Mostly termites

Location: Americas

Also called wind scorpions, sun spiders live underneath rotting tree bark. They have huge fangs that they use to kill and slice up their prey.

VELVET MITE

FAST FACTS

Class: Arachnida

Order: Acari

Family: Trombidiidae

Scientific name:
Unknown

Diet: Small insects

Location: Worldwide

Velvet mites emerge from the soil at certain times of the year to mate and to lay eggs, often just after a rain shower.

Dragonflies and Damselflies

AZURE DAMSELFLY

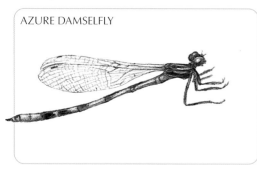

BLUE DASHER DRAGONFLY

FAST FACTS

Class: Insecta

Order: Odonata

Family: Coenagrionidae

Scientific name:
Coenagrion puella

Diet: Flying insects

Location: Eurasia, Africa

Azure damselflies live round sheltered fresh-water ponds, lagoons, and canals. They fly low over the water, catching insects on the wing.

FAST FACTS

Class: Insecta

Order: Odonata

Family: Libellulidae

Scientific name:
Pachydiplax longipennis

Diet: Flying insects

Location: North America

Blue dasher nymphs do not actively hunt prey, but feed on food as it passes by. Adults attack other insects from twig or rock perches.

BEAUTIFUL DEMOISELLE

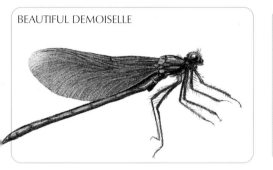

FAST FACTS

Class: Insecta

Order: Odonata

Family: Calopterygidae

Scientific name:
Calopteryx virgo

Diet: Flying insects

Location: Europe, Africa

The females of this species have metallic green bodies and golden brown wings. Males have blue bodies and dark, shiny wings.

DAWN DROPWING

FAST FACTS

Class: Insecta

Order: Odonata

Family: Libellulidae

Scientific name:
Trithemis aurora

Diet: Flying insects

Location: Asia

This dragonfly has a bright pink body and red-veined wings. This expert hunter catches flying insects in forests throughout Asia.

Cockroaches, Termites, and Mantids

SPINIFEX TERMITE

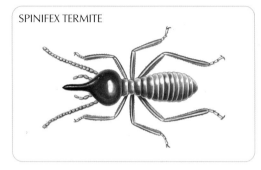

FAST FACTS

Class: Insects

Order: Isoptera

Family: Termitidae

Scientific name:
Nasutitermes triodiae

Diet: Dead wood

Location: Australia

These termites build huge mounds for their homes, that can reach 23 feet (7 m) high. Colonies of millions support a single queen.

GREEN BANANA ROACH

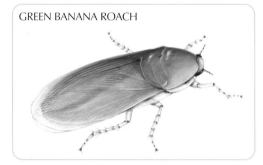

FAST FACTS

Class: Insecta

Order: Blattodea

Family: Blaberidae

Scientific name:
Panchlora nivea

Diet: Plant matter

Location: Caribbean

The green banana roach is a native of Cuba. It was introduced to the southern United States in shipments of fruit, such as bananas.

FLOWER MANTIS

The superb camouflage of this flower mantis allows it to hide among flower petals and pounce on unsuspecting prey.

FAST FACTS

Class: Insecta
Order: Mantodea
Family: Mantidae
Scientific name:
Unknown
Diet: Insects
Location: Tropical regions

273

Grasshoppers and Crickets

AUSTRALIAN PLAGUE LOCUST

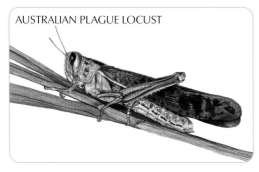

FIELD CRICKET

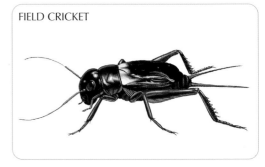

FAST FACTS

Class: Insecta

Order: Orthoptera

Family: Acrididae

Scientific name:
Chortoicetes terminifera

Diet: Plant matter

Location: Australia

Locusts are grasshopper-like insects that usually live by themselves. However, they sometimes join in huge swarms to form a plague.

FAST FACTS

Class: Insecta

Order: Orthoptera

Family: Gryllidae

Scientific name:
Gryllus campestris

Diet: Plants and animals

Location: Europe

This cricket is also known as the black cricket. Its long and powerful back legs help it hop through grass in the meadows where it lives.

TRUE KATYDID

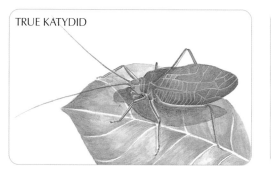

FAST FACTS

Class: Insecta
Order: Orthoptera
Family: Tettigoniidae
Scientific name:
Unknown
Diet: Tree leaves
Location: Worldwide

Katydids are named because of the sound males make when they call. Both males and females squawk loudly when disturbed.

GREAT GREEN BUSH-CRICKET

FAST FACTS

Class: Insecta
Order: Orthoptera
Family: Tettigoniidae
Scientific name:
Tettigonia viridissima
Diet: Plant matter
Location: Europe

These large crickets can grow up to 2 inches (5 cm) long. Males can be heard calling out for a mate in the summertime.

Bugs

COTTON STAINER BUG

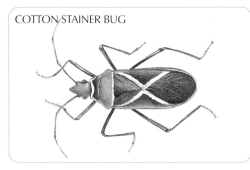

WATER CRICKET

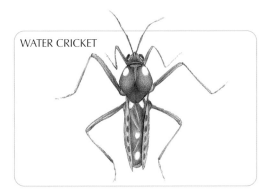

FAST FACTS

Class: Insecta

Order: Hemiptera

Family: Pyrrhocoridae

Scientific name:

Dysdercus decussatus

Diet: Sea hibiscus seeds

Location: Asia

These brightly colored bugs eat only the seeds of the sea hibiscus plant. They live in clusters underneath the plant's leaves.

FAST FACTS

Class: Insecta

Order: Hemiptera

Family: Veliidae

Scientific name:

Velia caprai

Diet: Insects

Location: Europe

Water crickets live in ponds and lakes. They scoot along the surface film of the water as they hunt, because they are light enough not to sink.

LARGE MILKWEED BUG

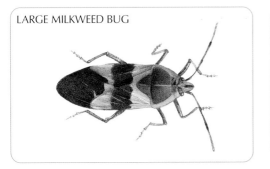

LACE BUG

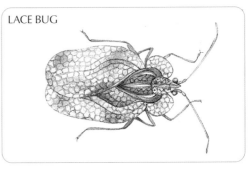

FAST FACTS

Class: Insecta

Order: Hemiptera

Family: Lygaeidae

Scientific name:
Oncopeltus fasciatus

Diet: Milkweed plants

Location: North America

This bug feeds on milkweed seeds. The poison in the seeds is transferred to the bug. Its bright colors show that it is dangerous.

FAST FACTS

Class: Insecta

Order: Hemiptera

Family: Tingidae

Scientific name:
Stephanitis pyri

Diet: Plant matter, fruit

Location: Eurasia

The delicate net of veins on these bugs' wings looks like lace. Sometimes called pear bugs, they can be pests in orchards, as they eat fruit.

Beetles

LONG-HORNED BEETLE

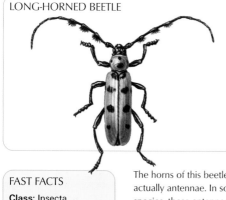

FAST FACTS

Class: Insecta

Order: Coleoptera

Family: Cerambycidae

Scientific name:
Unknown

Diet: Pollen, nectar, sap

Location: Worldwide

The horns of this beetle are actually antennae. In some species, these antennae can be many times longer than the rest of their body.

ROVE BEETLE

FAST FACTS

Class: Insecta

Order: Coleoptera

Family: Staphylinidae

Scientific name:
Unknown

Diet: Carrion insects

Location: Worldwide

The rove beetle is small and slender, perfect for squeezing between twigs and leaves as it hunts for food among the leaf litter.

EUPHOLUS WEEVIL

FAST FACTS

Class: Insecta

Order: Coleoptera

Family: Curculionidae

Scientific name:
Eupholus bennetti

Diet: Plant matter

Location: New Guinea

These weevils have bright colors and patterns, and are about 1 inch (2.5 cm) long. They live in the tropical rain forests of New Guinea.

TEN-SPOTTED LADYBUG

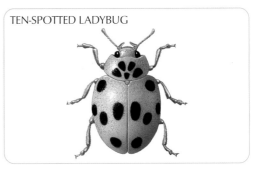

FAST FACTS

Class: Insecta

Order: Coleoptera

Family: Coccinellidae

Scientific name:
Coelophora pupillata

Diet: Insects, mites

Location: Asia

Ladybugs eat aphids, mealybugs, scale insects, spider mites, and other pests. They are often called the "gardener's friend."

Beetles

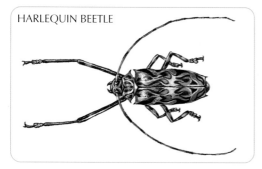

HARLEQUIN BEETLE

FAST FACTS

Class: Insecta

Order: Coleoptera

Family: Cerambycidae

Scientific name:
Acrocinus longimanus

Diet: Tree sap

Location: South Amercia

The eggs of this brilliantly colored tropical beetle are laid within the bark of fig trees. They chew their way out, then feed on sap.

TORTOISE BEETLE

FAST FACTS

Class: Insecta

Order: Coleoptera

Family: Chrysomelidae

Scientific name:
Unknown

Diet: Plant matter

Location: Worldwide

The round, curved bodies of these beetles look like tortoises. Some have bright colors and are used to decorate traditional jewelry.

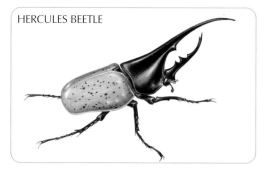

HERCULES BEETLE

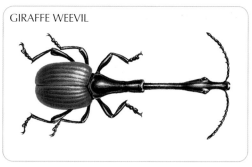

GIRAFFE WEEVIL

FAST FACTS

Class: Insecta

Order: Coleoptera

Family: Scarabaeidae

Scientific name:
Dynastes hercules

Diet: Rotting plants

Location: South America

These beetles can grow to more than 7 inches (18 cm) long. Their large horn, which is used in fighting, can be half of this length.

FAST FACTS

Class: Insecta

Order: Coleoptera

Family: Curculionidae

Scientific name:
Trachelopharus giraffe

Diet: Plant matter

Location: Madagascar

The tapering thorax and long, extended head may help this giraffe weevil to feed. It can grow up to 3 inches (7.5 cm) long.

Beetles

FIRE BEETLE

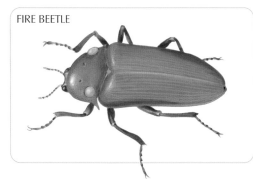

The fire beetle has two spots on its thorax and one on its abdomen. These produce a natural light that is the brightest of any beetle.

FAST FACTS

Class: Insecta

Order: Coleoptera

Family: Elateridae

Scientific name:

Pyrophorus noctilucus

Diet: Dung

Location: South America

RHINOCEROS DUNG BEETLE

This dung beetle has a horn on the front of its head that looks like a rhinoceros horn. It can be found in grasslands and also in rural areas.

FAST FACTS

Class: Insecta

Order: Coleoptera

Family: Scarabaeidae

Scientific name:

Oxysternon conspicillatum

Diet: Dung

Location: South America

CONVERGENT LADYBUG

FAST FACTS

Class: Insecta

Order: Coleoptera

Family: Coccinellidae

Scientific name:
Hippodamia convergens

Diet: Insects, mites

Location: Americas

These ladybugs are so good at eating aphids that they are sold as a natural pest control. They have up to 13 spots on their abdomen.

SOUTH AMERICAN STAG BEETLE

FAST FACTS

Class: Insecta

Order: Coleoptera

Family: Lucanidae

Scientific name:
Chiasognathus grantii

Diet: Leaves, nectar

Location: South America

This stag beetle is common in Chile and Argentina. Male stag beetles have enormous jaws that they use in mating contests.

Flies

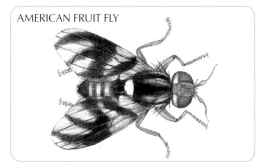

AMERICAN FRUIT FLY

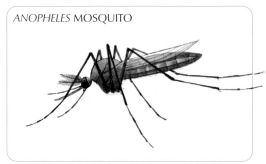

ANOPHELES MOSQUITO

FAST FACTS

Class: Insecta

Order: Diptera

Family: Tephritidae

Scientific name:
Rhagoletis pomonella

Diet: Fruit

Location: North America

The larva (or maggot) of this fly is called the apple maggot because it burrows into apples to feed. This spoils the fruit for eating.

FAST FACTS

Class: Insecta

Order: Diptera

Family: Culicidae

Scientific name:
Anopheles sp.

Diet: Blood

Location: Warm regions

Only the female *Anopheles* mosquito transmits malaria. This is a disease caused by a parasite in her saliva, which is transferred when she bites.

ROBBER FLY

The robber fly is the most active predator of all the flies. It can suck its victim completely dry of its body fluids in seconds.

FAST FACTS

Class: Insecta

Order: Diptera

Family: Asilidae

Scientific name:

Unknown

Diet: Flying insects

Location: Dry regions

Butterflies and Moths

ANISE SWALLOWTAIL

88 BUTTERFLY

FAST FACTS

Class: Insecta

Order: Lepidoptera

Family: Papilionidae

Scientific name:
Papilio sp.

Diet: Plant matter

Location: North America

This butterfly can be seen in open grassland and vacant lots. The young caterpillars eat leaves, while the older ones eat flowers.

FAST FACTS

Class: Insecta

Order: Lepidoptera

Family: Nymphalidae

Scientific name:
Diaethria sp.

Diet: Rotting fruit, dung

Location: South America

These small South American butterflies have a distinctive "88" underneath their wings. The topside can be shimmering blue or green.

PIPEVINE SWALLOWTAIL

FAST FACTS

Class: Insecta
Order: Lepidoptera
Family: Papilionidae
Scientific name:
Battus philenor
Diet: Nectar
Location: North America

Adult pipevine swallowtails are drawn to the California pipevine plant to feed and to lay their eggs underneath the plant's leaves.

BORDERED PATCH BUTTERFLY

FAST FACTS

Class: Insecta
Order: Lepidoptera
Family: Nymphalidae
Scientific name:
Chlosyne lacinia
Diet: Nectar
Location: Americas

This butterfly is common in both deserts and grasslands. It has very small front legs, and walks only on its middle and back legs.

Butterflies and Moths

YELLOW EMPEROR MOTH

FAST FACTS

Class: Insecta

Order: Lepidoptera

Family: Saturniidae

Scientific name:
Saturnia pavoria

Diet: Adults do not feed

Location: Eurasia

This is one of Europe and Asia's largest moths. The colorful males fly only by day, and find the night-flying females by their scent.

WHITE-LINED SPHINX MOTH

FAST FACTS

Class: Insecta

Order: Lepidoptera

Family: Sphingidae

Scientific name:
Hyles lineata

Diet: Nectar

Location: America

Adult white-lined sphinx moths' wings can be longer than 5 inches (13 cm). They flap their wings quickly and hover like hummingbirds.

CERISY'S SPHINX MOTH

FAST FACTS

Class: Insecta

Order: Lepidoptera

Family: Sphingidae

Scientific name:
Smerinthus cerisyi

Diet: Nectar

Location: North America

This butterfly prefers to live near rivers or low-lying ground near willows. Its larvae feed on willow and poplar trees.

CURRANT CLEARWING

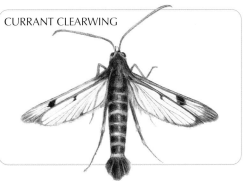

FAST FACTS

Class: Insecta

Order: Lepidoptera

Family: Sesiidae

Scientific name:
Synanthedon tipuliformis

Diet: Plant matter

Location: Europe

Clearwing moths lose the scales on their wings, so they are clear. These moths are pests because they feed on currant bushes.

Butterflies and Moths

GHOST MOTH

FAST FACTS

Class: Insecta

Order: Lepidoptera

Family: Hepialidae

Scientific name:
Aenetus dulcis

Diet: Adults do not feed

Location: Australia

The adult lives of ghost moths are devoted to reproduction. Females of this species are green, while males are white.

ELIENA SKIPPER

FAST FACTS

Class: Insecta

Order: Lepidoptera

Family: Hesperiidae

Scientific name:
Trapezites eliena

Diet: Plant matter

Location: Australia

Skippers are named because they dart rapidly from flower to flower. This species has clubbed and hooked antennae.

INDIAN LUNA MOTH

FAST FACTS

Class: Insecta

Order: Lepidoptera

Family: Saturniidae

Scientific name:
Actias selene

Diet: Plant matter

Location: Asia

This large and graceful moth is a member of the giant silkworm moth family. Females of this species are larger than males.

GIANT OWL BUTTERFLY

FAST FACTS

Class: Insecta

Order: Lepidoptera

Family: Nymphalidae

Scientific name:
Caligo idomeneus

Diet: Rotting fruit

Location: South America

The large eyespot on the underside of this moth's back wings scares predators. The topside of its wings is a shimmery blue.

Bees, Wasps, and Ants

DOMESTIC HONEYBEE

HAIRY-LEGGED MINING BEES

FAST FACTS

Class: Insecta

Order: Hymenoptera

Family: Apidae

Scientific name:
Apis mellifera

Diet: Nectar

Location: Worldwide

While this bee was originally found only in Europe, it has been bred all over the world for its honey. It usually feeds honey to its young.

FAST FACTS

Class: Insecta

Order: Hymenoptera

Family: Andrenidae

Scientific name:
Dasypoda hirtipes

Diet: Nectar

Location: Europe

Female mining bees dig holes in the ground in which they lay their eggs, and store pollen balls and nectar in individual cells.

LEAF-CUTTER ANTS

These voracious ants live in the tropical forests of the Americas. They may chew more than 10 percent of all leaves in these forests.

FAST FACTS

Class: Insecta

Order: Blattodea

Family: Formicidae

Scientific name:

Atta sp.

Diet: Fungus

Location: Americas

Bees, Wasps, and Ants

SCOLIID WASP

AMERICAN PELECINID WASP

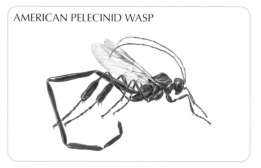

FAST FACTS

Class: Insecta

Order: Hymenoptera

Family: Scoliidae

Scientific name:
Scolia procer

Diet: Nectar, pollen

Location: Southeast Asia

A female scoliid wasp digs into the soil to find scarab beetle grubs. She paralyzes them, then lays a single egg inside the grubs.

FAST FACTS

Class: Insecta

Order: Hymenoptera

Family: Pelecinidae

Scientific name:
Pelecinus polyturator

Diet: Nectar

Location: Americas

The larvae of these wasps are parasites of beetle larvae. Females have a long, slender abdomen used to seek out the beetle hosts.

RUBY-TAILED WASP

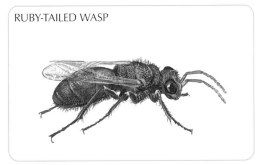

FAST FACTS

Class: Insecta

Order: Hymenoptera

Family: Chrysididae

Scientific name:
Chrysis ignita

Diet: Nectar

Location: Europe

These wasps are also called cuckoo wasps because they lay their eggs in the nests of other insects. Their larvae feed on the nests' food.

ROSE CYNIPID

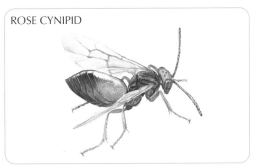

FAST FACTS

Class: Insecta

Order: Hymenoptera

Family: Cynipidae

Scientific name:
Diplolepis rosae

Diet: Rose plants

Location: Worldwide

Tiny rose cynipids lay their eggs in rose bushes. These hatch to form larvae. There can be a mass of 50 larvae sharing the same branch.

Other Insects

EAST DOBSONFLY

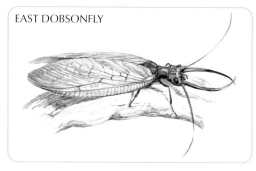

FAST FACTS

Class: Insecta

Order: Megaloptera

Family: Corydalidae

Scientific name:

Corydalis cornutus

Diet: Adults do not feed

Location: North America

Dobsonflies spend most of their lives as aquatic larvae feeding on other insects. The adults only live long enough to breed.

MAYFLY

FAST FACTS

Class: Insecta

Order: Ephemeroptera

Family: Ephemeridae

Scientific name:

Ephemera vulgata

Diet: Adults do not feed

Location: Europe

Adult mayflies live for one day. The aquatic nymphs feed on plants. Mayflies are the only insects that molt after they have wings.

STONEFLY

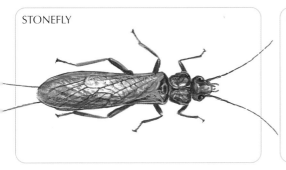

FAST FACTS

Class: Insecta

Order: Plecoptera

Family: Perlidae

Scientific name:
Perla burmeisteriana

Diet: Adults may not feed

Location: Central Europe

This stonefly can reach over 1 inch (25 mm) in length. The aquatic nymph feeds on other insects and is very sensitive to polluted water.

GRAIN THRIP

FAST FACTS

Class: Insecta

Order: Thysanoptera

Family: Thripidae

Scientific name:
Limothrips cerealium

Diet: Cereals, grains

Location: Warm regions

Thrips belong to the order Thysanoptera, which means "fringed wing." Grain thrips suck the sap from the ears of cereals, and can be pests.

Other Insects

SILVERFISH

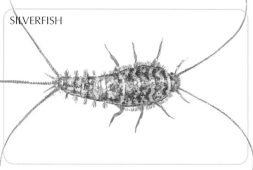

HUMAN FLEA

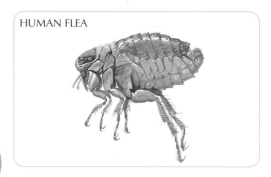

FAST FACTS

Class: Insecta

Order: Thysanura

Family: Lepismatidae

Scientific name:

Lepismodes iniquilinus

Diet: Organic matter

Location: Worldwide

Silverfish have antennae on their heads, plus three long tails extending from their abdomen. This one can eat paper and starchy material.

FAST FACTS

Class: Insecta

Order: Siphonaptera

Family: Pulicidae

Scientific name:

Pulex irritans

Diet: Blood

Location: Worldwide

Parasitic fleas have lost the power of flight. Instead they can leap onto their mammal hosts using their powerful back legs.

BOOK LOUSE

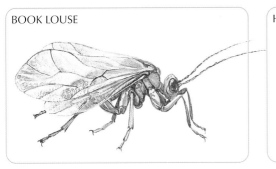

FAST FACTS

Class: Insecta
Order: Pscoptera
Family: Ectopsocidae
Scientific name:
Ectopsocus briggsi
Diet: Plant matter
Location: Worldwide

Book lice have discovered just how tasty paste and book bindings are. They feed on these as well as on plant matter.

HEAD LOUSE

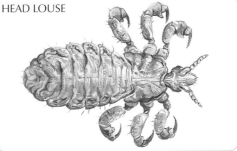

FAST FACTS

Class: Insecta
Order: Phthiraptera
Family: Pediculidae
Scientific name:
Pediculus capitis
Diet: Blood
Location: Worldwide

Head lice are wingless insect parasites that occur specifically in human hair. Their eggs, called nits, are attached to hairs.

Classifying Bugs

The way in which bugs are classified is constantly changing. Only the major orders and families are listed below. Families are listed in alphabetical order. Not all bugs have common names, so there are some gaps.

CLASS INSECTA	**INSECTS**
ORDER THYSANURA	**SILVERFISH**
Lepismatidae	Silverfish (firebrats)
ORDER EPHEMEROPTERA	**MAYFLIES**
Baetidae	Small mayflies
Ephemerellidae	Midboreal mayflies
Ephemeridae	Burrowing mayflies
Heptageniidae	Stream mayflies
Leptophlebiidae	Spinners
ORDER ODONATA	**DRAGONFLIES and DAMSELFLIES**
Aeschnidae	Darners
Calopterygidae	Broad-winged damselflies
Coenagrionidae	Narrow-winged damselflies

Cordulegastridae	Biddies
Corduliidae	Green-eyed skimmers
Gomphidae	Clubtails
Lestidae	Spread-winged damselflies
Libellulidae	Common skimmers
Macromiidae	Cruisers
Petaluridae	Graybacks
ORDER BLATTODEA	**COCKROACHES**
Blaberidae	
Blattellidae	
Blattidae	Common cockroaches
ORDER MANTODEA	**MANTIDS**
Empusidae	
Hymenopodidae	Flower mantids
Mantidae	Common praying mantids
ORDER ISOPTERA	**TERMITES**
Hodotermitidae	Rotten-wood termites
Kalotermitidae	Damp-wood termites
Mastotermitidae	
Rhinotermitidae	Subterranean termites
Termitidae	Nasutiform termites
ORDER DERMAPTERA	**EARWIGS**
Chelisochidae	Black earwigs
Forficulidae	Common earwigs

Labiduridae — Long-horned earwigs
Labiidae — Little earwigs

ORDER PLECOPTERA — STONEFLIES

Capniidae — Small winter stoneflies
Chloroperlidae — Green stoneflies
Isoperlidae — Green-winged stoneflies
Leuctridae — Rolled-winged stoneflies
Nemouridae — Spring stoneflies
Peltoperlidae — Roachlike stoneflies
Perlidae — Common stoneflies
Perlodidae — Perlodid stoneflies
Pteronarcidae — Giant stoneflies
Taeniopterygidae — Winter stoneflies

ORDER ORTHOPTERA — GRASSHOPPERS and CRICKETS

Acrididae — Short-horned grasshoppers
Cooloolidae — Cooloola monster
Cylindrachetidae — Sand gropers
Eneopterinae — Bush crickets
Eumastacidae; Tanaoceridae — Monkey grasshoppers
Gryllacrididae; Rhaphidophoridae — Leaf-rolling crickets, camelcrickets, cave crickets
Gryllidae — True crickets
Gryllotalpidae — Mole crickets
Myrmecophilidae — Ant crickets

Stenopelmatidae — King crickets
Tetrigidae — Pygmy grasshoppers
Tettigoniidae — Long-horned grasshoppers and katydids
Tridactylidae — Pygmy mole crickets

ORDER PHASMATODEA — STICK AND LEAF INSECTS

Phasmatidae — Stick insects
Phylliidae — Leaf insects
Timemidae — Timemas

ORDER PHTHIRAPTERA — PARASITIC LICE

Boopiidae
Echinophthiriidae — Spiny sucking lice
Gyropidae — Guinea pig lice
Haematopinidae — Mammal-sucking lice
Hoplopleuridae
Laemobothriidae — Bird lice
Linognathidae — Smooth sucking lice
Menoponidae — Poultry-chewing lice
Pediculidae — Human lice
Philopteridae — Feather-chewing lice
Ricinidae — Bird lice
Trichodectidae — Mammal-chewing lice

ORDER HEMIPTERA — BUGS

Achilidae — Achilid planthoppers
Adelgidae — Pine aphids

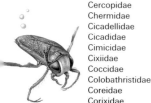

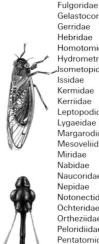

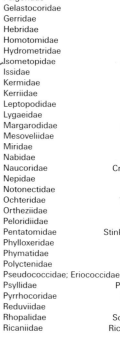

Aleyrodidae	Whiteflies
Alydidae	Broad-headed bugs
Anthocoridae	Flower bugs, minute pirate bugs
Aphididae	Aphids
Aphrophoridae	
Aradidae	Flat bugs, bark bugs
Asterolecaniidae	Pit scales
Belostomatidae	Giant water bugs
Berytidae	Stilt bugs
Carsidaridae	
Cercopidae	Spittlebugs and froghoppers
Chermidae	Pine and spruce aphids
Cicadellidae	Leafhoppers
Cicadidae	Cicadas
Cimicidae	Bed bugs
Cixiidae	Cixiid planthoppers
Coccidae	Soft scales, wax scales
Colobathristidae	
Coreidae	Leaf-footed bugs, crusader bugs
Corixidae	Water boatmen
Cydnidae	Negro bugs
Dactylopiidae	Cochineal bugs
Delphacidae	Delphacid planthoppers
Derbidae	Derbid planthoppers
Diaspididae	Armored scale insects
Dictyopharidae	Dictyopharid planthoppers
Dinidoridae	
Dipsocoridae; Schizopteridae	Jumping ground bugs
Eriosomatidae	Woolly and gall-making aphids
Eurymelidae; Membracidae	Treehoppers
Flatidae	Flatid planthoppers

Fulgoridae	Fulgorids
Gelastocoridae	Toad bugs
Gerridae	Water striders
Hebridae	Velvet water bugs
Homotomidae	
Hydrometridae	Water measurers
Isometopidae	Jumping tree bugs
Issidae	Issid planthoppers
Kermidae	Gall-like coccids
Kerriidae	Lac insects
Leptopodidae	Spiny shore bugs
Lygaeidae	Seed bugs
Margarodidae	Giant scale insects
Mesoveliidae	Water treaders
Miridae	Leaf or plant bugs
Nabidae	Damsel bugs
Naucoridae	Creeping water bugs
Nepidae	Waterscorpions
Notonectidae	Backswimmers
Ochteridae	Velvety shore bugs
Ortheziidae	Ensign scales
Peloridiidae	Moss bugs
Pentatomidae	Stink bugs, shield bugs
Phylloxeridae	Gall aphids
Phymatidae	Ambush bugs
Polyctenidae	Bat bugs
Pseudococcidae; Eriococcidae	Mealybugs
Psyllidae	Psyllids, lerp insects
Pyrrhocoridae	Red bugs, stainers
Reduviidae	Assassin bugs
Rhopalidae	Scentless plant bugs
Ricaniidae	Ricaniid planthoppers

Saldidae	Shore bugs
Scutelleridae	Jewel bugs, shield-backed bugs
Tessaratomidae	
Tettigarctidae	Hairy cicadas
Tingidae	Lace bugs
Triozidae	
Veliidae	Ripple bugs

ORDER NEUROPTERA — **NET-VEINED INSECTS**

Ascalaphidae	Owlflies
Chrysopidae	Green lacewings
Coniopterygidae	Dusty-wings
Hemerobiidae	Brown lacewings
Ithonidae	Moth lacewings
Mantispidae	Mantidflies
Myrmeleontidae	Antlions
Nemopteridae	
Polystoechotidae	Giant lacewings
Psychopsidae	Silky lacewings
Sisyridae	Spongeflies

ORDER COLEOPTERA — **BEETLES**

Anobiidae	Furniture beetles
Anthribidae	Fungus weevils
Bostrichidae	Branch and twig borers, auger beetles
Brentidae	Primitive weevils
Bruchidae	Seed beetles
Buprestidae	Metallic wood-boring beetles, jewel beetles

Cantharidae	Soldier beetles
Carabidae	Ground beetles
Cerambycidae	Longhorn beetles, longicorn beetles
Chrysomelidae	Leaf beetles
Cicindelidae	Tiger beetles
Cleridae	Checkered beetles
Coccinellidae	Ladybird beetles
Cucujidae	Flat bark beetles
Curculionidae	Snout beetles and weevils
Dermestidae	Dermestid beetles
Dytiscidae	Predacious diving beetles
Elateridae	Click beetles
Erotylidae	Pleasing fungus beetles
Gyrinidae	Whirligig beetles
Haliplidae	Crawling water beetles
Histeridae	Hister beetles
Hydrophilidae	Water scavenger beetles
Laemophloeidae	
Lampyridae	Fireflies, lightning bugs
Lathridiidae	Minute brown scavenger beetles
Lucanidae	Stag beetles
Lycidae	Net-winged beetles
Lymexylidae	Ship-timber beetles
Meloidae	Blister beetles
Melyridae	Softwinged flower beetles
Mycetophagidae	Hairy fungus beetles
Nitidulidae	Nitidulid beetles
Passalidae	Passalid beetles or bessbugs
Psephenidae	Water pennies

Ptiliidae	Feather-winged beetles
Ptinidae	Spider beetles
Pyrochroidae	Fire-colored beetles
Rhipiphoridae	Rhipiphoridan beetles
Scarabaeidae	Scarab beetles
Scolytidae	Bark and ambrosia beetles
Silphidae	Carrion beetles
Silvanidae	Flat grain beetles
Staphylinidae	Rove beetles
Tenebrionidae	Darkling beetles
Trogidae	Carcass beetles
Trogositidae	Bark-gnawing beetles

ORDER SIPHONAPTERA — FLEAS

Dolichopsyllidae; Ceratophyllidae	Rodent fleas
Leptopsyllidae	Mouse fleas
Pulicidae	Common fleas
Tungidae	Sticktight and chigoe fleas

ORDER DIPTERA — FLIES

Acroceridae	Bladder flies
Agromyzidae	Leafminer flies
Anthomyiidae	Root maggot flies
Apioceridae	Flower-loving flies
Asilidae	Robber flies
Bibionidae	March flies
Blephariceridae	Net-winged midges
Bombyliidae	Bee flies
Braulidae	Beelice
Calliphoridae	Blowflies
Canacidae	Beach flies
Cecidomyiidae	Gall midges

Ceratopogonidae	Punkies, biting midges
Chaoboridae	Phantom midges
Chironomidae	Midges
Chloropidae	Grass flies
Coelopidae	Seaweed flies
Conopidae	Thick-headed flies
Culicidae	Mosquitoes
Dolichopodidae	Long-legged flies
Drosophilidae	Vinegar (pomace) flies
Empididae	Dance flies, water cruisers
Ephydridae	Shore flies
Fanniidae	
Fergusoninidae	Eucalyptus flies
Heleomyzidae	Sun flies
Hippoboscidae	Louse flies and sheep keds
Lonchaeidae	Lance flies
Micropezidae	Stilt-legged flies
Muscidae	House flies and bushflies
Mycetophilidae	Fungus gnats
Mydidae	Mydas flies
Nemestrinidae	Tanglevein flies
Neriidae	Cactus flies
Neurochaetidae	Upside-down flies
Nycteribiidae; Streblidae	Bat flies
Oestridae; Gasterophilidae	Botflies
Phoridae	Scuttle flies
Piophilidae	Skipper flies
Platypezidae	Flat-footed flies
Platystomatidae	Platystomatid flies
Psychodidae	Moth flies
Ptychopteridae	Phantom crane flies

Pyrgotidae	Pyrgotid flies
Rhagionidae	Snipe flies
Sarcophagidae	Flesh flies
Scenopinidae	Window flies
Sciaridae	Black fungus gnats
Sciomyzidae	March flies
Sepsidae	Ant flies
Simuliidae	Black or sand flies
Sphaeroceridae	Short heel flies, small dung flies
Stratiomyidae	Soldier flies
Syrphidae	Hover flies
Tabanidae	Horse and deer flies
Tachinidae	Tachinid flies
Tephritidae	Fruit flies
Teratomyzidae	Fern flies
Therevidae	Stiletto flies
Tipulidae	Crane flies
Trichoceridae	Winter crane flies

ORDER TRICHOPTERA CADDISFLIES

Hydropsychidae	Net-spinning caddisflies
Leptoceridae	Long-horned caddisflies
Limnephilidae	Northern caddisflies
Phryganeidae	Large caddisflies
Psychomyiidae	Tube-making caddisflies

ORDER LEPIDOPTERA BUTTERFLIES AND MOTHS

Alucitidae	Many-plume moths
Anthelidae	

Apaturidae	Hackberry and goatweed butterflies
Arctiidae	Tiger moths
Bombycidae	Silkworm moths
Bucculatricidae	
Carposinidae	Carposinid moths
Carthaeidae	
Castniidae	
Citheroniidae	Royal moths
Coleophoridae	Casebearer moths
Cosmopterygidae	
Copromorphidae	
Cossidae	Wood moths
Ctenuchidae	Ctenuchid moths
Danaidae	Milkweed butterflies
Drepanidae	Hook-tip moths
Eupterotidae; Zanolidae	Zanolid moths
Gelechiidae	Gelechiid moths
Geometridae	Measuringworm moths, loopers
Gracilariidae	Leaf blotch miners
Hepialidae	Ghost moths, swifts
Hesperiidae	Skippers
Incurvariidae	Yucca moths
Lasiocampidae	Tent caterpillar and lappet moths
Libytheidae	Snout butterflies
Limacodidae	
Lycaenidae	Gossamer-winged butterflies
Lymantriidae	Tussock moths
Lyonetiidae	Lyonetiid moths

305

Noctuidae	Noctuids
Notodontidae	Prominents
Nymphalidae	Brush-foots
Oecophoridae	Oecophorid moths
Papilionidae	Swallowtails
Pieridae	Whites and sulfurs
Plutellidae	Diamondback moths
Psychidae	Bagworm moths
Pterophoridae	Plume moths
Pyralidae	Pyralid moths
Riodinidae	Metalmarks
Saturniidae	Giant silkworm moths
Satyridae	Satyrs, nymphs, and arctics
Sesiidae	Clear-winged moths
Sphingidae	Sphinx or hawk moths
Thaumetopoeidae	
Tineidae	Clothes moths
Tortricidae	Tortricid moths
Uraniidae	
Yponomeutidae	Ermine moths
Zygaenidae	Smoky moths

ORDER HYMENOPTERA   BEES, ANTS, WASPS, AND SAWFLIES

Agaonidae	Fig wasps
Andrenidae	Andrenid bees
Apidae	Digger bees, carpenter bees, cuckoo bees, bumblebees, honeybees
Argidae	Argid sawflies
Braconidae	Braconids
Cephidae	Stem sawflies
Chalcididae	Chalcids

Chrysididae	Cuckoo wasps
Cimbicidae	Cimbicid sawflies
Colletidae	Yellow-faced and plasterer bees
Cynipidae	Gall wasps
Encyrtidae	Encyrtid wasps
Eulophidae; Aphelininae	Eulophid wasps
Eurytomidae	Seed chalcids
Evaniidae	Hatchet wasps
Formicidae	Ants
Halictidae	Sweat (halictid) bees
Ibaliidae	Ibaliid wasps
Ichneumonidae	Ichneumonids
Megachilidae	Leaf-cutting bees
Melittidae	Melittid bees
Mutillidae	Velvet ants
Mymaridae	Fairy wasps
Pelecinidae	Pelecinids
Pergidae	Pergid sawflies
Pompilidae	Spider wasps
Pteromalidae	Pteromalid wasps
Scelionidae	Scelionid wasps
Scoliidae	Scoliid wasps
Siricidae	Horntails
Sphecidae	Sphecid wasps
Stephanidae	Stephanid wasps
Tenthredinidae	Common sawflies
Tiphiidae	Tiphid wasps
Torymidae	Torymid wasps
Vespidae	Vespid wasps

CLASS ARACHNIDA ARACHNIDS

ORDER ARANEAE	SPIDERS
Agelenidae	Funnel weavers
Antrodiaetidae	Folding trap-door spiders
Araneidae	Orb weavers
Clubionidae	Sac spiders
Ctenidae	Wandering spiders
Ctenizidae	Trap-door spiders
Dictynidae	Dictynid spiders
Dipluridae	Funnel-web spiders
Eresidae	Eresid spiders
Heteropodidae	Huntsman spiders
Linyphiidae	Dwarf spiders
Loxoscelidae	Violin spiders
Lycosidae	Wolf spiders
Oxyopidae	Lynx spiders
Pholcidae	Daddy-long-legs spiders
Pisauridae	Fisher spiders
Salticidae	Jumping spiders
Scytodidae	Spitting spiders
Selenopidae	Selenopid crab spiders
Sparassidae	Huntsman spiders
Tetragnathidae	Large-jawed orb weavers
Theraphosidae	Tarantulas
Theridiidae	Comb-footed spiders
Thomisidae	Crab spiders

ORDER SCORPIONES	SCORPIONS
Buthidae	Buthid scorpions
Iuridae	Iurid scorpions

ORDER PSEUDOSCORPIONES	PSEUDO-SCORPIONS
Cheliferidae	
Chernetidae	Chernetids

ORDER OPILIONES	HARVESTMEN
Leiobunidae	
Phalangiidae	

ORDER ACARI	MITES AND TICKS
Argasidae	Soft ticks
Hydrachnellae	Water mites
Ixodidae	Hard ticks
Tetranychidae	Spider mites
Trombidiidae	Velvet mites

ORDER UROPYGI	WHIPSCORPIONS
Thelyphonidae	Vinegaroons

ORDER AMBLYPYGI	TAILLESS WHIPSCORPIONS
Phrynidae	Tarantulidae

ORDER SOLIFUGAE	WINDSCORPIONS OR SUNSPIDERS
Eremobatidae	
Solpugidae	

Glossary

abdomen The part of an animal's body that contains the digestive system and the organs of reproduction.

antennae Delicate sense organs on an insect's head, which it uses to smell, touch, taste, or hear the world.

arachnid An arthropod with four pairs of legs, a body divided into two parts, chelicerae, and simple eyes.

arthropod An animal with jointed legs and a body divided into segments covered by an exoskeleton.

ballooning A method used by spiders to travel long distances. They are carried on the wind as they dangle from a long strand of silk.

camouflage The colors or patterns that help hide an animal so that it blends in with its environment.

cephalothorax The head and thorax of arachnids are combined in this body region. The chelicerae, pedipalps, and the eight legs are attached to it, and it also holds a spider's brain and sucking stomach.

chelicera (pl. chelicerae) A spider's fang used for injecting venom into prey. In other arachnids they are pincer-like for shredding prey.

chrysalis The pupa of a butterfly or a moth.

cocoon A protective case, usually made of silk. Insects make cocoons to keep themselves safe while they are pupae, before emerging as adults.

colony A group of animals of the same species that live and work together to survive.

compound eye An insect's main pair of eyes, made up of many small eyes, each of which forms part of the image in the insect's brain.

courtship The behavior of animals that ultimately results in mating.

disguise The method an animal uses to imitate a part of its environment.

dragline A thread of silk attached to an object that a spider will trail behind it as it moves around.

egg sac A silk covering woven by a female spider to wrap up her eggs, to protect them, and keep them from drying out.

elytra A beetle's forewings. These two wings provide a protective covering for the beetle's delicate pair of flying wings underneath.

environment All the natural features of Earth, such as landforms and climate, that affect living things.

evolution The changes in plants and animals over many years as they adapt to new conditions.

exoskeleton The hard, outer skeleton of an arthropod, which supports the muscles and soft internal organs.

ganglia A cluster of nerve cells. In many invertebrates, ganglia control different parts of the body.

gill An organ that absorbs oxygen from water. Gills are found in many aquatic animals, including insects.

habitat The home of an animal or plant. There can be many habitats within the one environment.

halteres The modified back wings of a fly. They help the fly to balance during flight.

host An animal that is attacked by a parasite.

invertebrate An animal that has no backbone. Some invertebrates have soft bodies, but others, like arthropods, are protected and supported by their hard exoskeletons.

labium An insect's lower lip. It protects the piercing stylets of sucking insects.

larva (pl. larvae) The immature stage of some insects that looks completely different from their parents.

lift The upward force that helps flying animals to stay in the air.

metamorphosis The transformation of a juvenile insect (a nymph or a larva) into an adult.

midgut Nutrients from food are absorbed here.

migration A group of animals traveling from one region to another, to breed or to find enough food to eat in winter or summer.

mimicry A strategy by which an animal copies or imitates another animal, either to hunt or to avoid being hunted.

molt The process in insects and spiders of shedding the exoskeleton to grow or to change into adults.

nymph A life stage of some insects. Nymphs are often similar to adults, but do not have fully developed wings.

ocellus (pl. ocelli) A small, light-sensitive eye. Many insects have three ocelli on the top of their head, which help flying insects stay level in flight.

ovary Female reproductive organ where eggs are produced.

ovipositor A tube at the tip of a female insect's abdomen used for laying eggs.

parasite An organism that lives on or in another organism (called the host) from which it derives its nourishment.

pedipalp An appendage on the cephalothorax of arachnids, used to touch, taste, smell, and hold prey. Male spiders use these to deposit sperm.

pollen Tiny grains produced by the male part of a flower that will fertilize the eggs in the female part of a flower.

pollinate To transfer pollen from the male reproductive organs of a plant to the female organs of a same plant.

predator An animal that hunts or preys on other animals for its food.

prey An animal that is hunted by predators.

pupa A stage that many insects undergo during metamorphosis. Inside a pupal case, its juvenile body parts break down and adult features emerge.

reproduction The process by which plants and animals make new life.

scavenger An animal that feeds on rotting organic matter, like food scraps, dung, and dead animals.

silk A strong but elastic substance produced by many insects and spiders. Silk is liquid until it leaves the animal's body.

species Plants and animals that display features in common. When they breed, they produce offspring that can also breed.

sperm Male reproductive cell that fertilizes the egg.

spigots Tubes that spin spider silk into strands.

spinnerets Two to six finger-like organs at the tip of a spider's abdomen. Different types of silk made by the spider emerge from the spinnerets.

spiracle A breathing hole in the side of an insect that takes oxygen into the body and expels waste gases, such as carbon dioxide.

stinger A hollow structure on the tail of insects and scorpions that pierces flesh and injects venom.

stylet A sharp mouthpart used for piercing food.

swarm A mass of insects, such as bees or locusts, that collect or move around together for eating, mating, or finding a new nest site.

thorax The middle section of an insect's body. It is full of muscles that drive the insect's wings and three pairs of legs, all of which are attached to the thorax.

trachea (pl. tracheae) A breathing tube. Insects and most spiders have a whole network of tracheae that carry oxygen to every organ and cell.

tympanum (pl. tympana) A membrane that acts like an ear. It receives sounds as vibrations in the air. This information is carried to the brain, so the insect can hear.

venom A chemical that is injected into another animal to kill, paralyze, or deter it from attacking. Venom can also help liquefy the prey so it can be sucked up.

vertebrate An animal with an internal skeleton, such as fish, amphibians, reptiles, birds, and mammals.

Index

Acknowledgments

PHOTOGRAPHIC CREDITS

Key t=top; l=left; r=right; tl=top left; tc=top center; tr=top right; cl=center left; c=center; cr=center right; b=bottom; bl=bottom left; bcl=bottom center left; bc=bottom center; bcr=bottom center right; br=bottom right

Ad-Libitum; APL/CBT = Australian Picture Library/Corbis; APL/MP = Australian Picture Library/Minden Pictures; AUS = Auscape International; BCC = Bruce Coleman Collection; COR = Corel Corp.; DS = Digital Stock; DV = Digital Vision; GI = Getty Images; MW = Mantis Wildlife; PD = Photodisc; PL = photolibrary.com; PPW = Premaphotos Wildlife; PR = Photo Researchers Inc.; SB = Stockbyte

2c SB 23cr COR 25c SB 26c DS l COR r DV 27c AUS 41c DV 45c DV 46bl PR 49tc DV 50bl DV 51c DV 52br COR 53c DS 57c COR 59c DV 63cl GI 84bl DV 86l AUS 87c DV 88l DV 89br DS 93l PPW r AUS 94l BCC 95c APL/CBT 97c PD 98c COR 102br MW l DV 103c PL 113c COR 114c PD 116b APL/CBT 119c AUS 126r SB 164bl COR r DV 168l COR 171c COR 172r COR 173l PD 175c DV 176bl PPW 180b AUS 186c PD 195c DV 200b BCC 204cr COR 208tr COR 209bc COR 213c COR 214bl APL/CBT 219l COR r AUS 223l APL/MP 229br, l APL/CBT 230l AUS r COR 235tl COR 236bl, br COR 237c AUS 238cr APL/CBT 241c AUS 243l PL 244bl AUS 245c AUS 246c AUS 247bl PD 249c DV 251c APL/CBT 252l Ad-Libitum/Mihal Kaniewski 253bl Ad-Libitum/Mihal Kaniewski 256c Ad-Libitum/Mihal Kaniewski 273cl AUS 285cl AUS 293cl DV

ILLUSTRATION CREDITS

Susanna Addario, Alistair Barnard, Andrew Beckett/ Illustration, Sally Beech, Anne Bowman, Martin Camm, Simone End, Christer Eriksson, Alan Ewart, Giuliano Fornari, Tim Hayward/ Bernard Thornton Artists UK, Robert Hynes, Jon Gittoes, Mike Gorman, Ray Grinaway, David Kirshner, Frank Knight, Angela Lober, Iain McKellar, Richard McKennar, James McKinnon, John Mac/ FOLIO, MagicGroup s.r.o. (Czech Republic) - www.magicgroup.cz, Rob Mancini, Colin Newman/ Bernard Thornton Artists UK, Nicola Oram, Tony Pyrzakowski, John Richards, Edwina Riddell, Barbara Rodanska, Trevor Ruth, Ngaire Sales, Claudia Saraceni, Kevin Stead, Thomas Trojer, Wildlife Art Ltd (B. Croucher, Sandra Doyle, Ian Jackson, Steve Roberts, Peter Scott, Chris Shields), Roger Swainston, Genevieve Wallace, Ann Winterbotham

INDEX

Puddingburn Publishing Services

CONSULTANT

Noel Tait was Associate Professor at the Department of Biological Sciences, Macquarie University, Sydney, Australia, and is now an independent consultant on invertebrate biology.